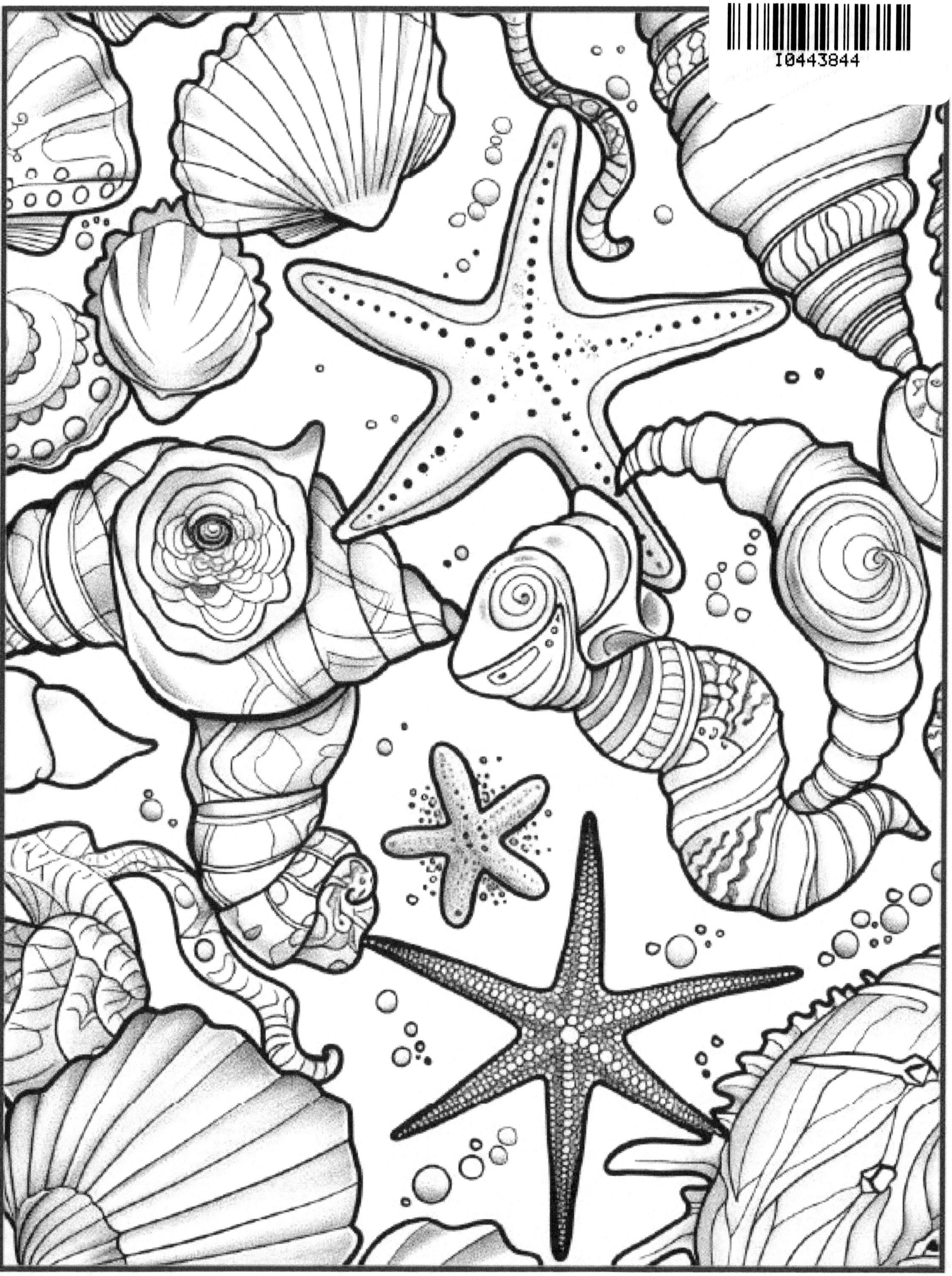

I0443844

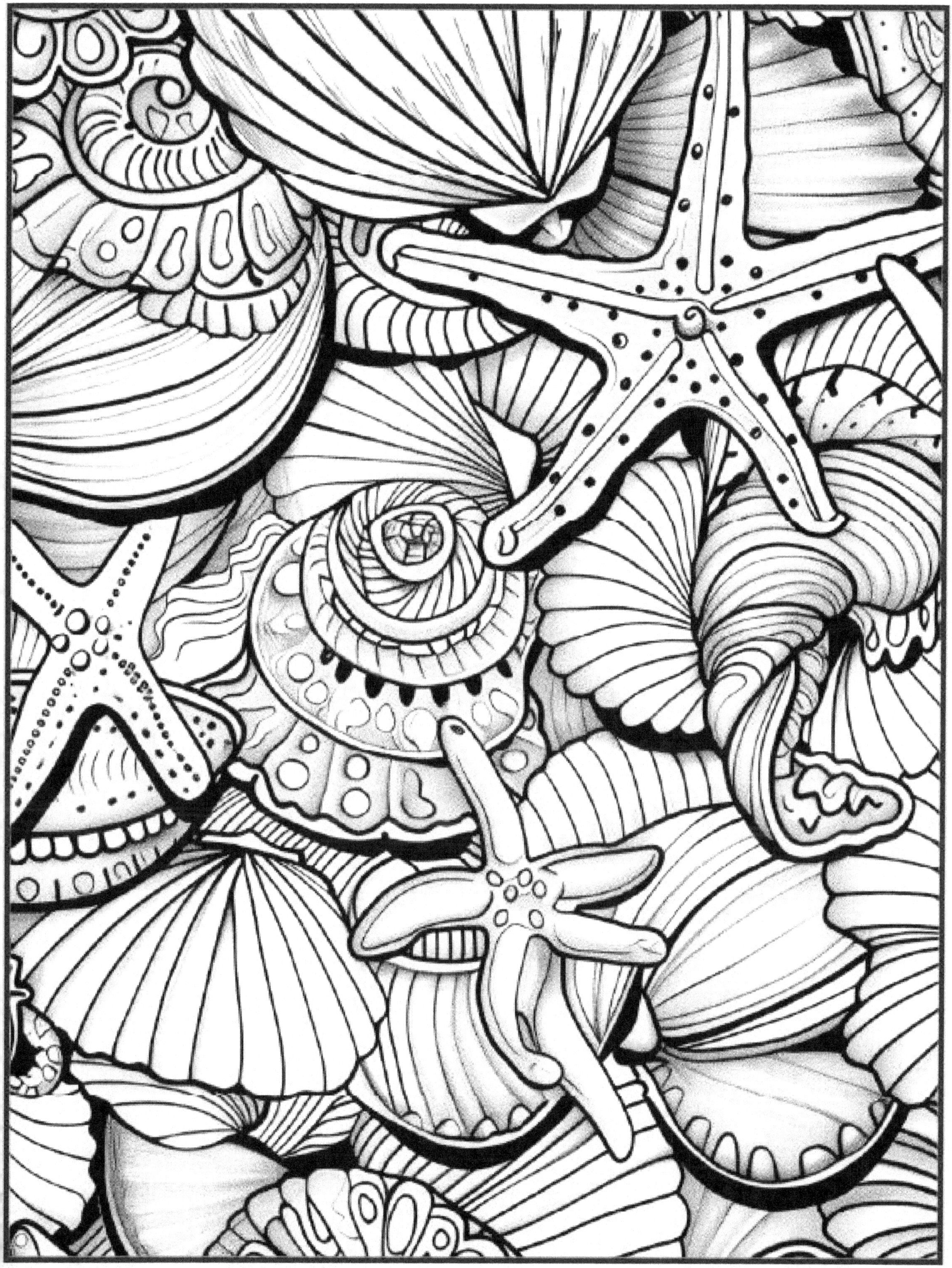

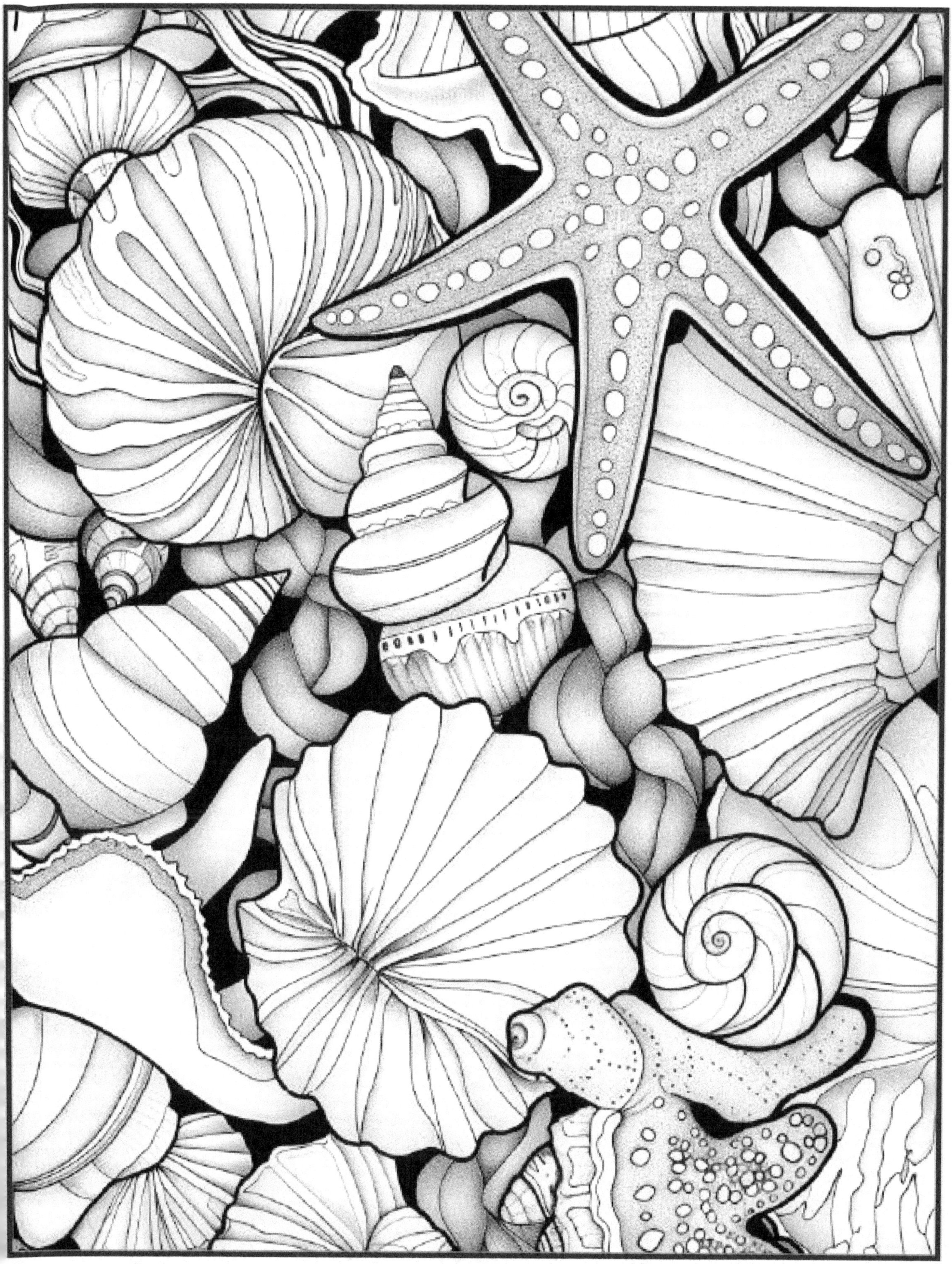

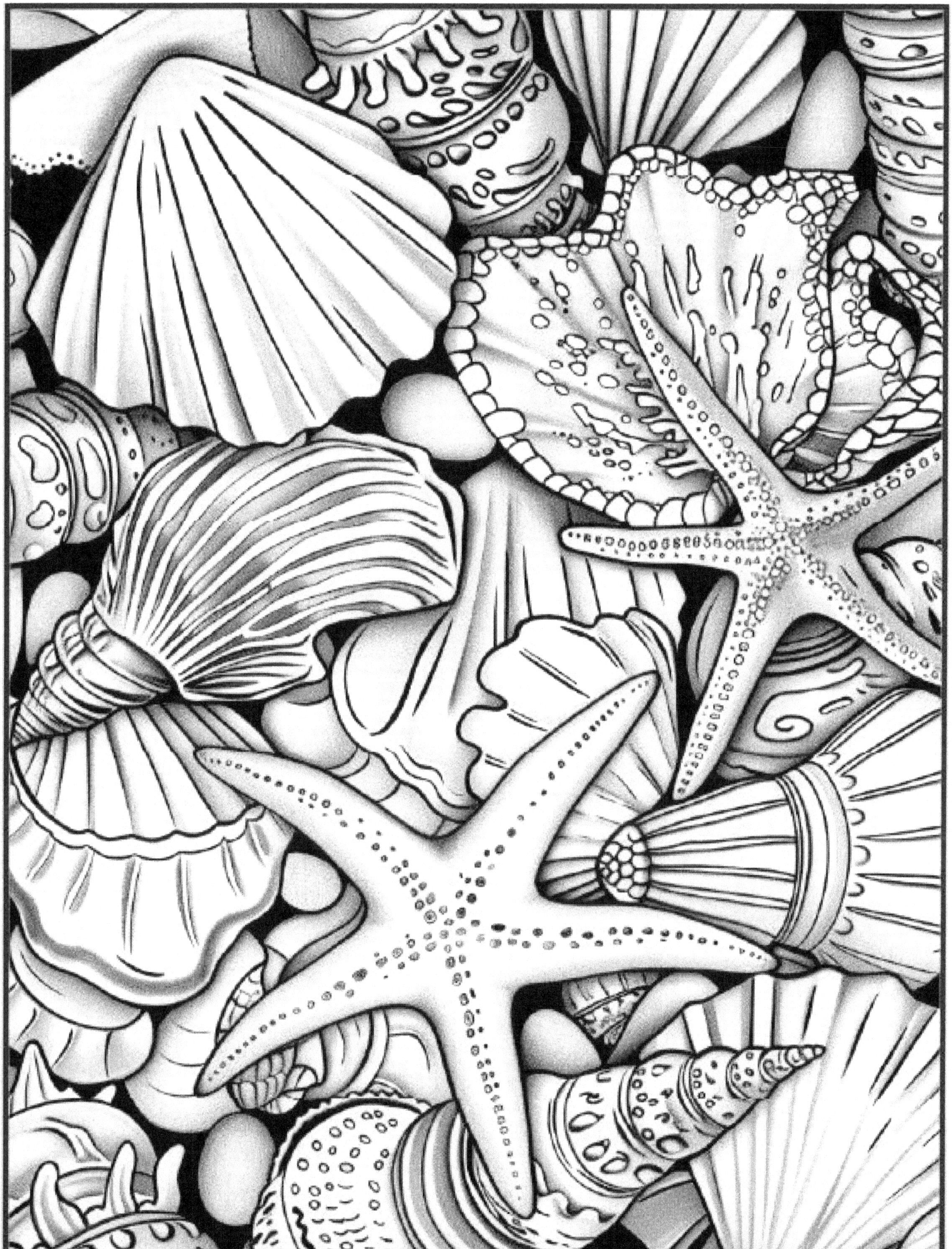

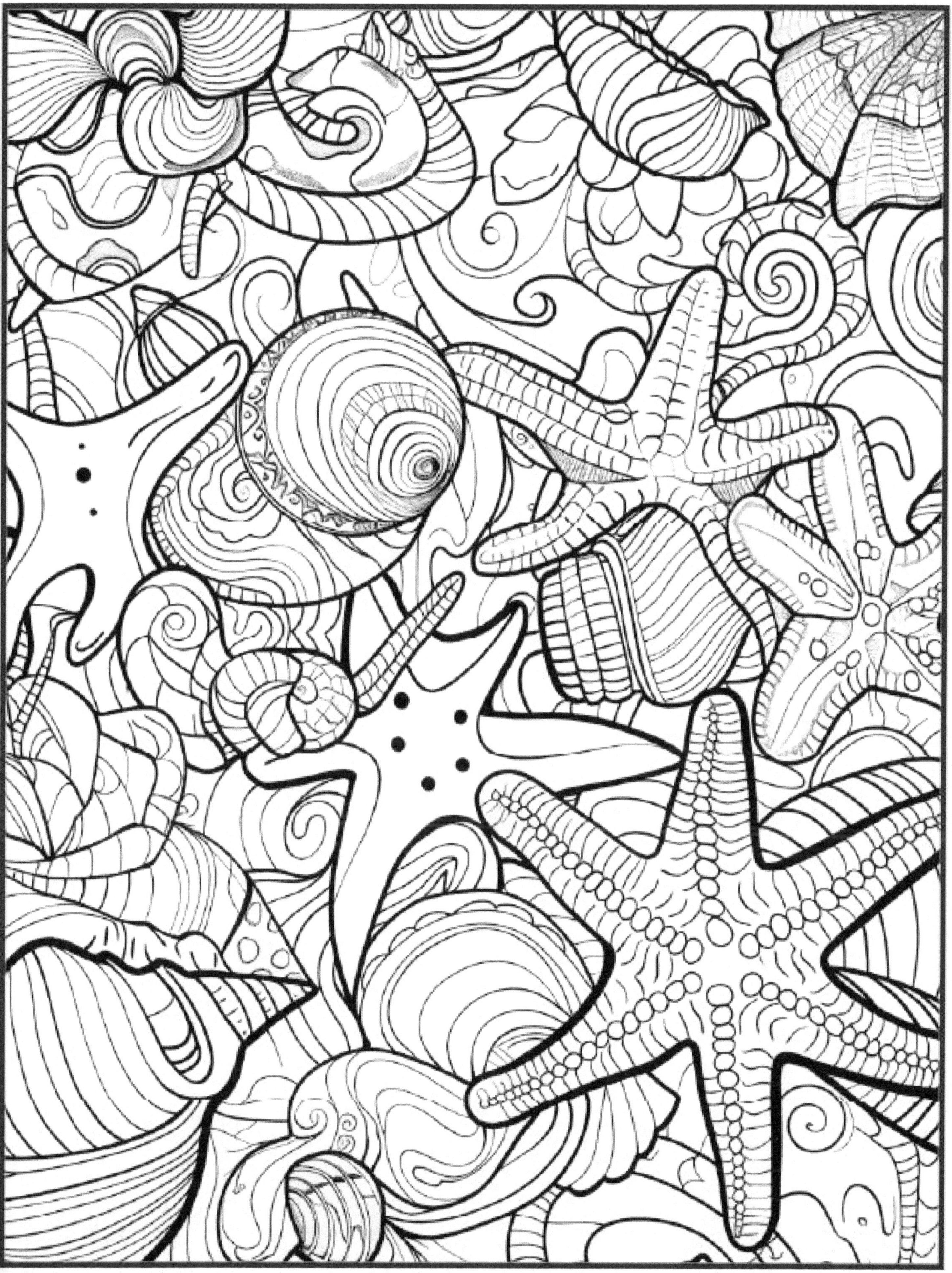

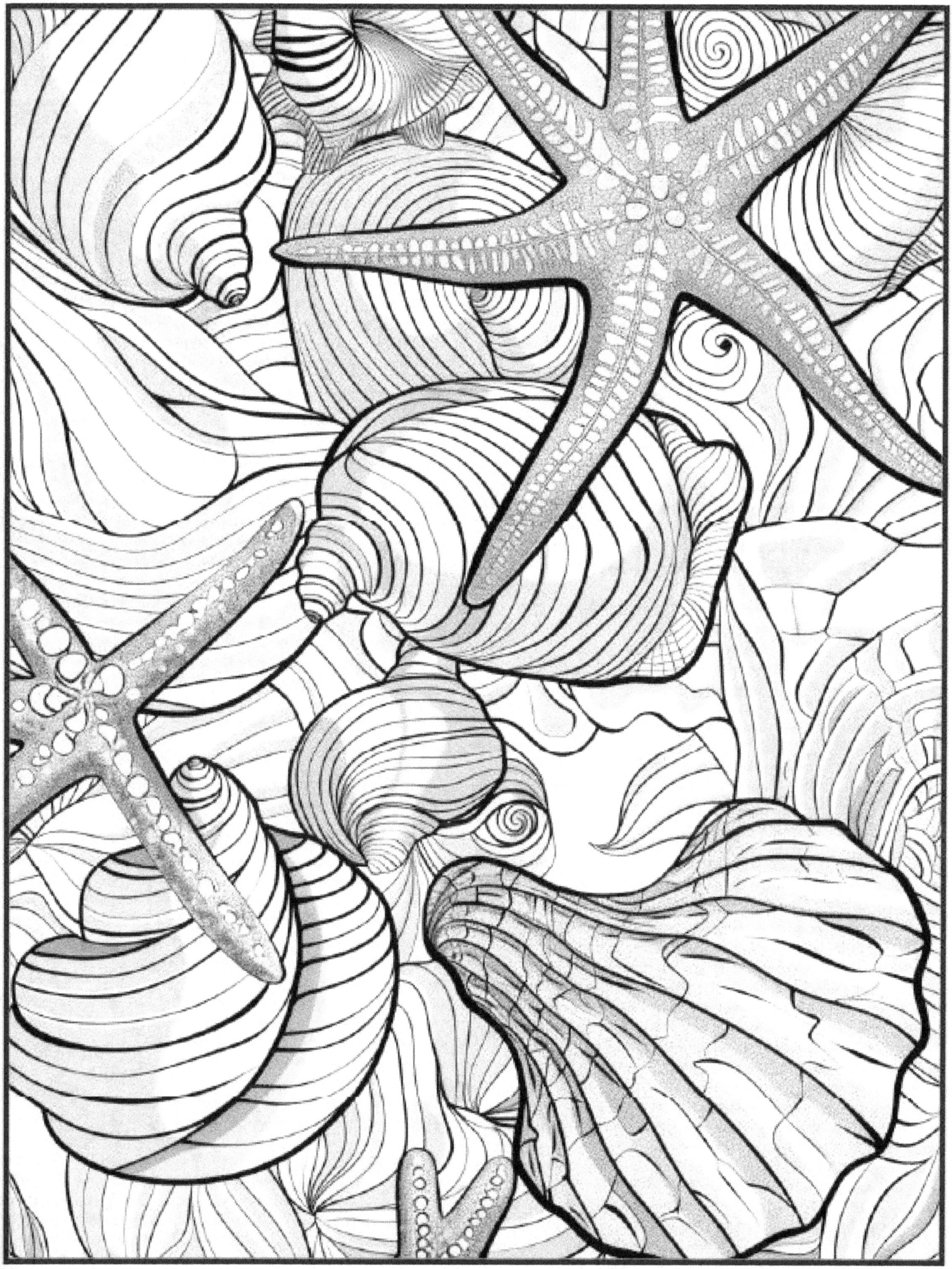

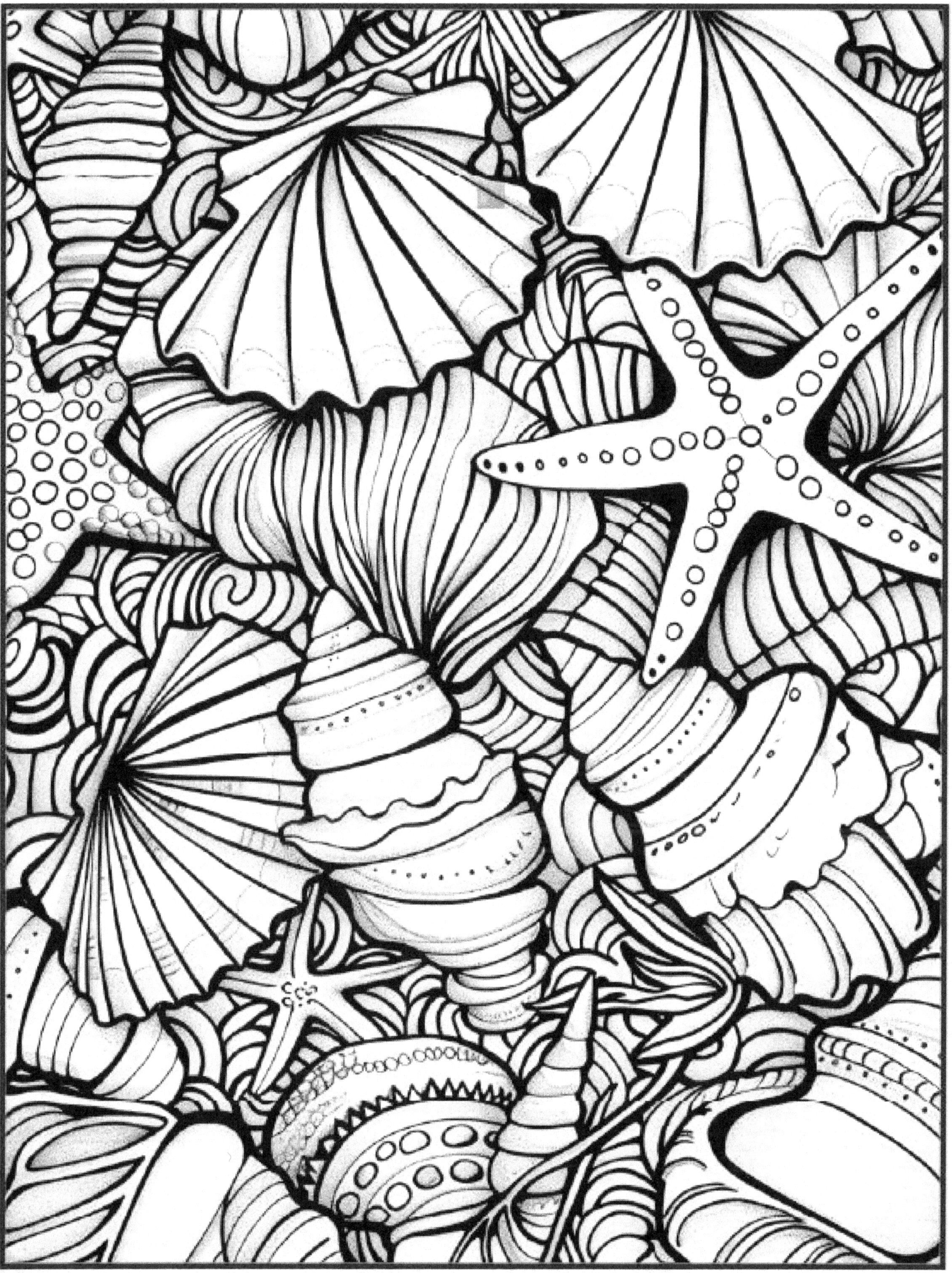

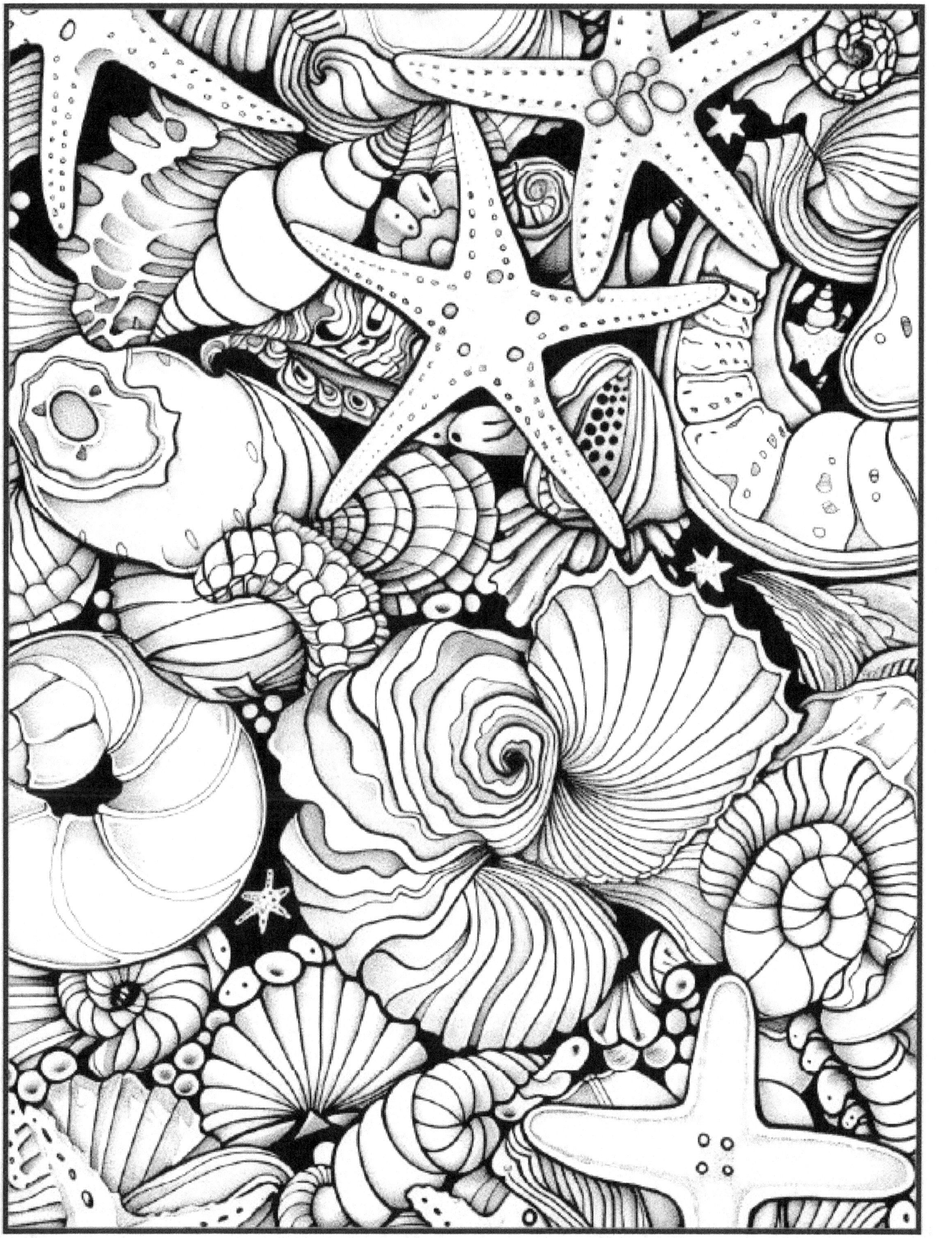

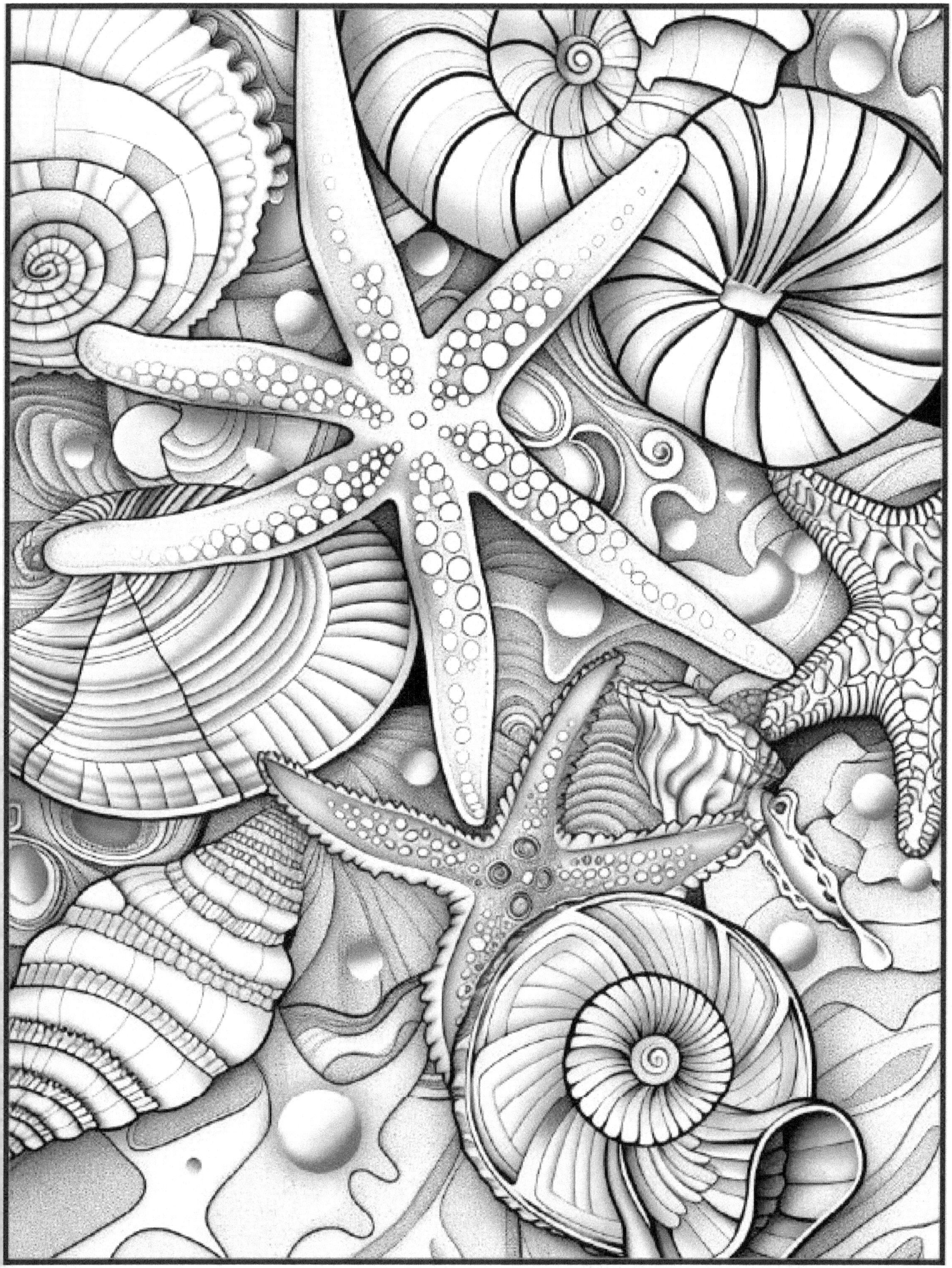

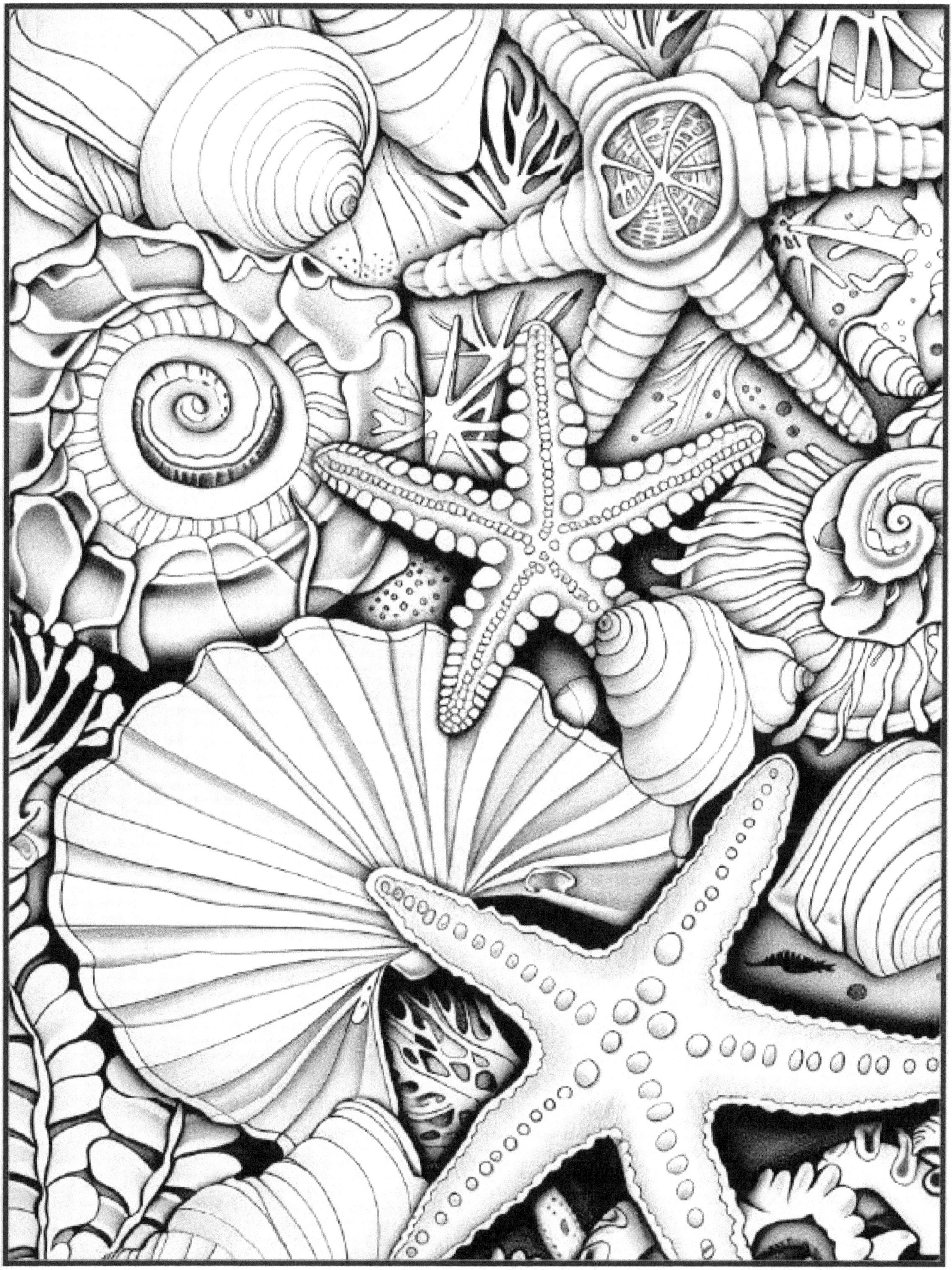

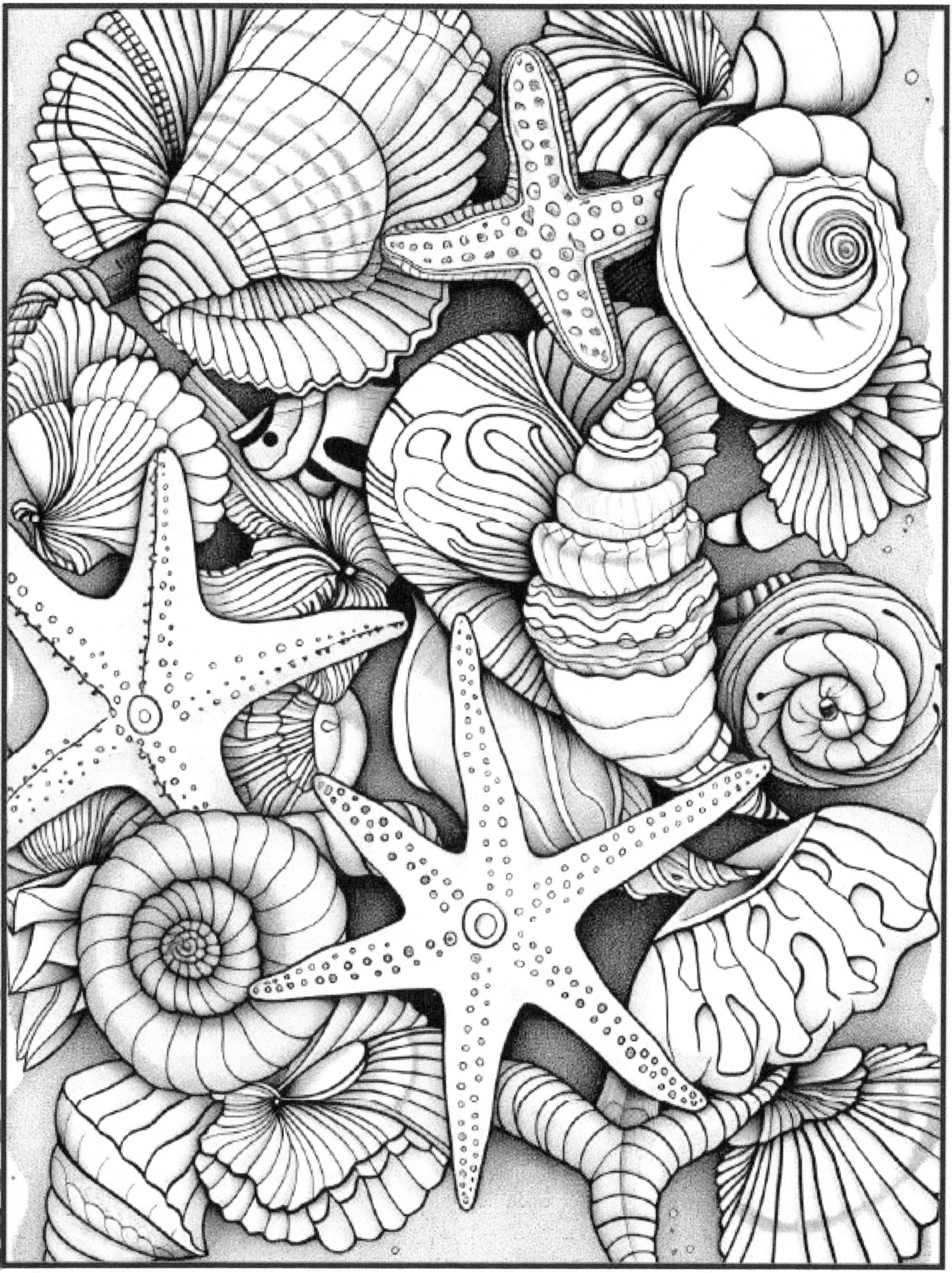

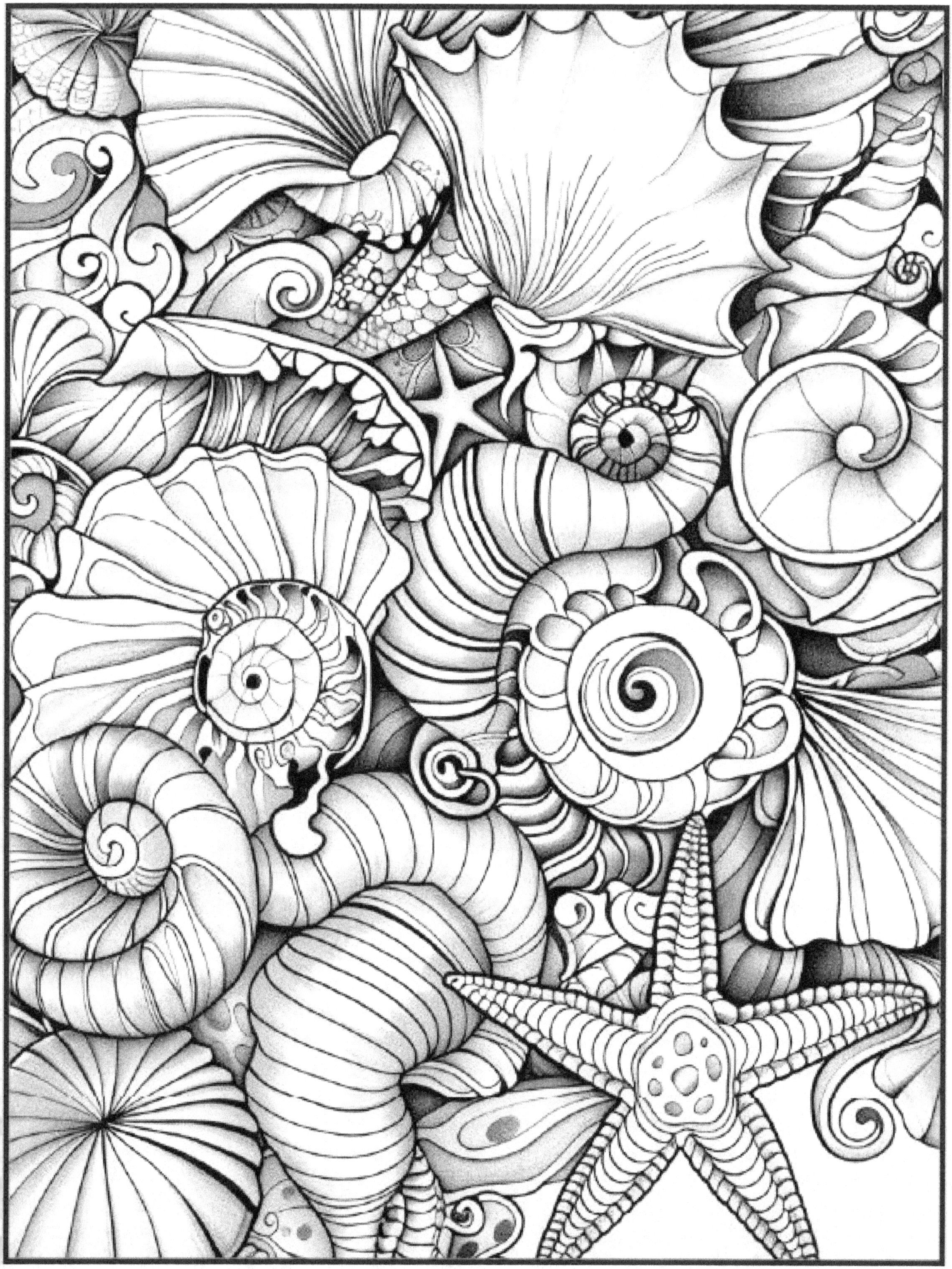

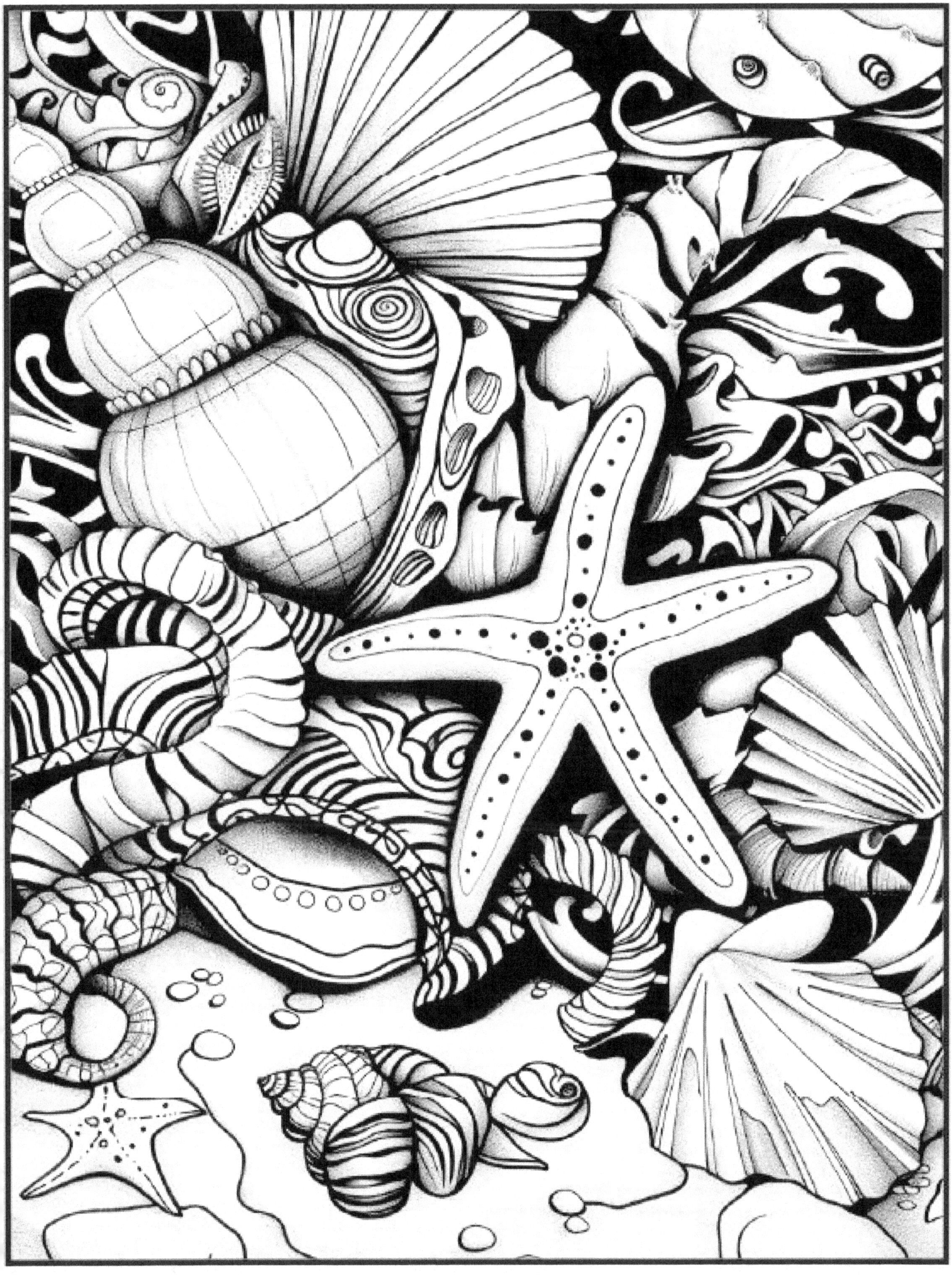

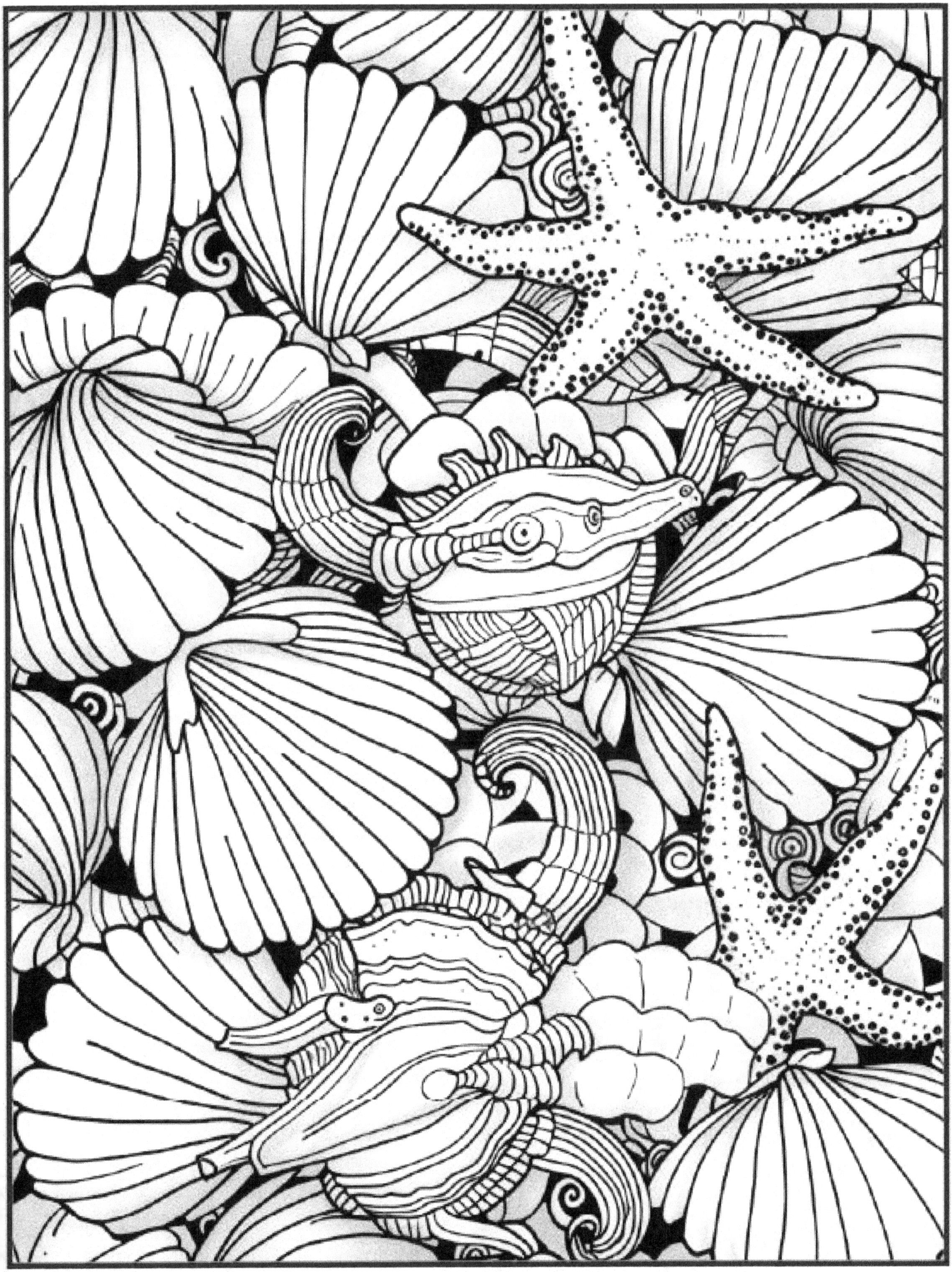

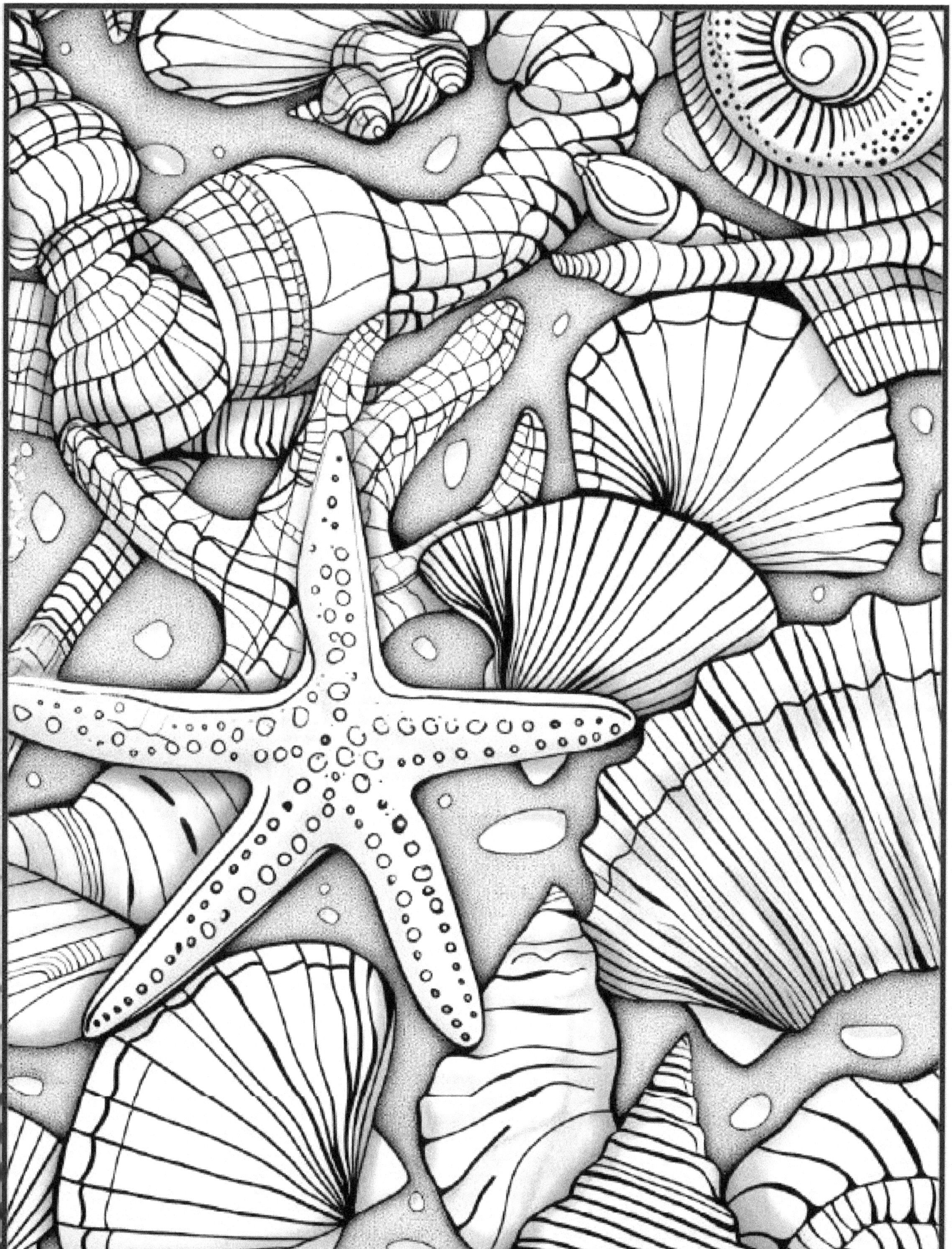

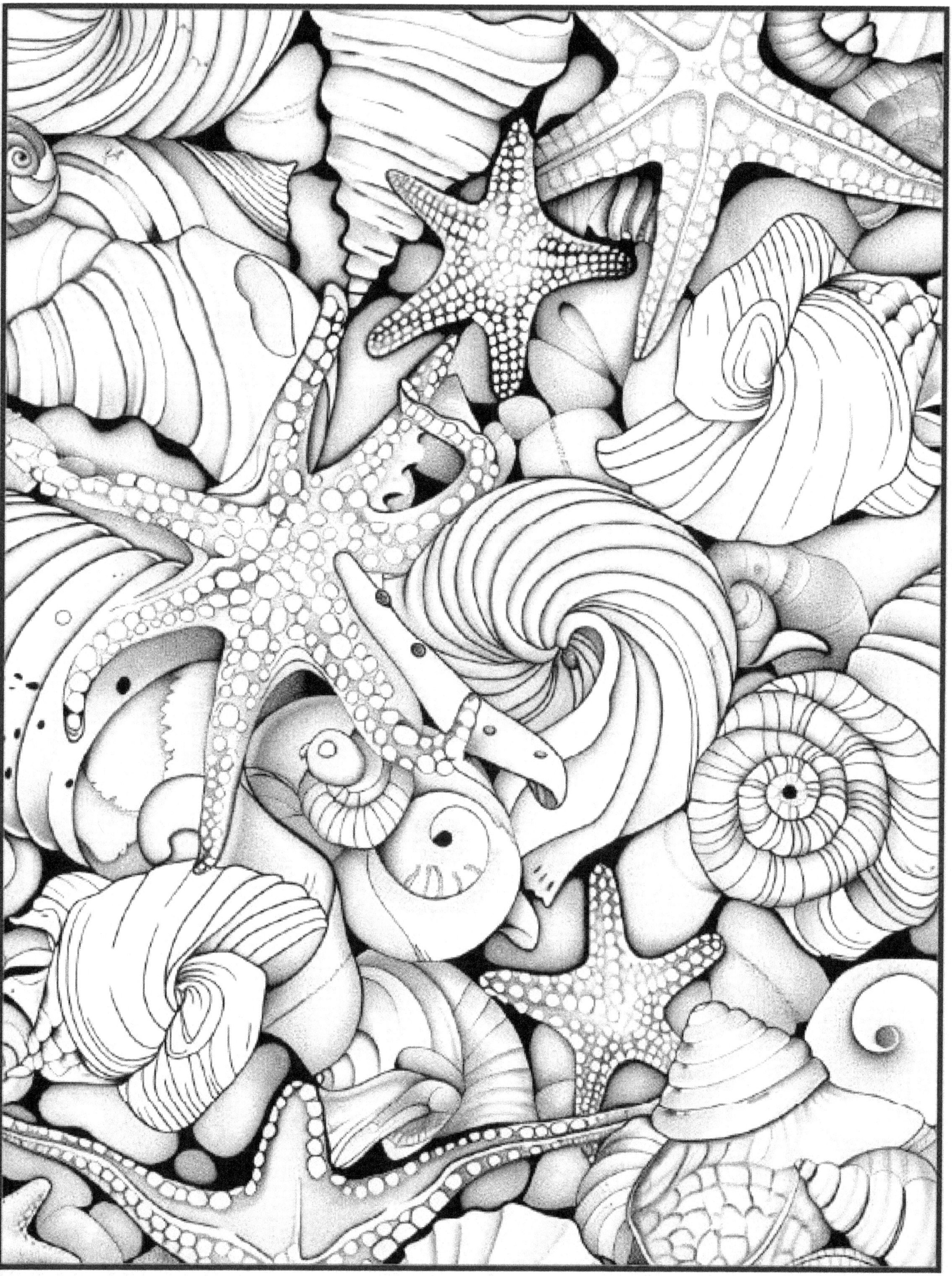

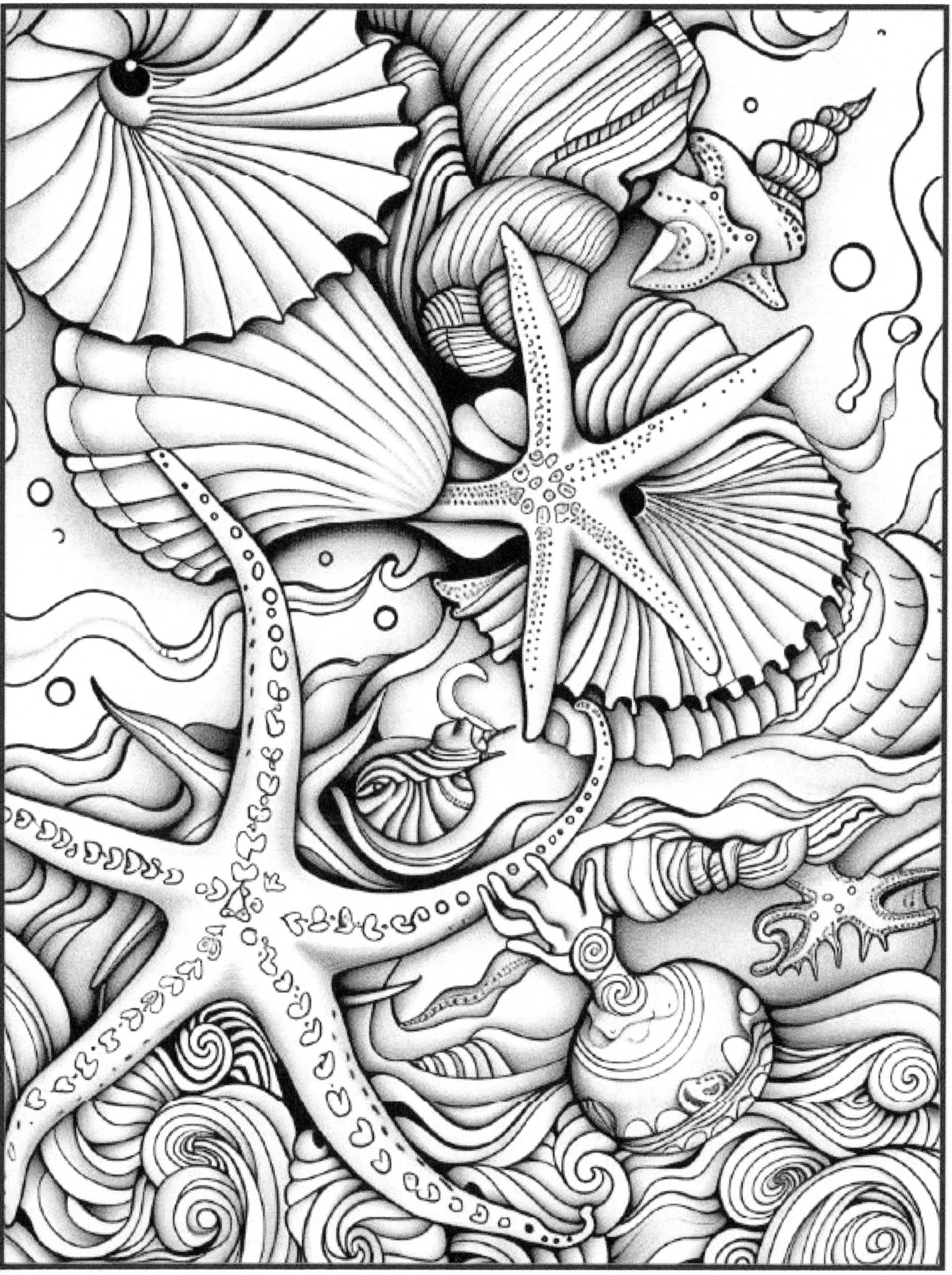

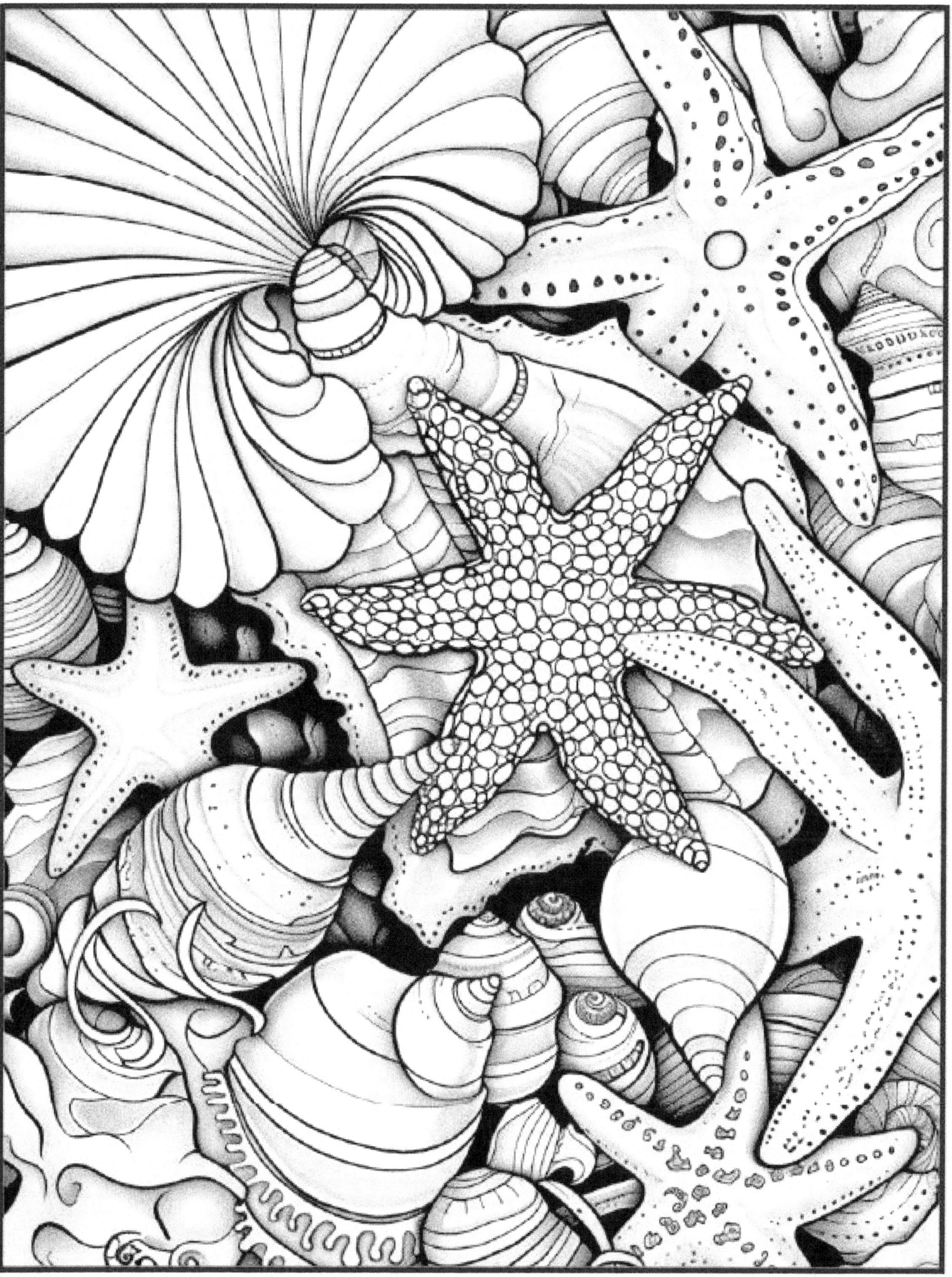

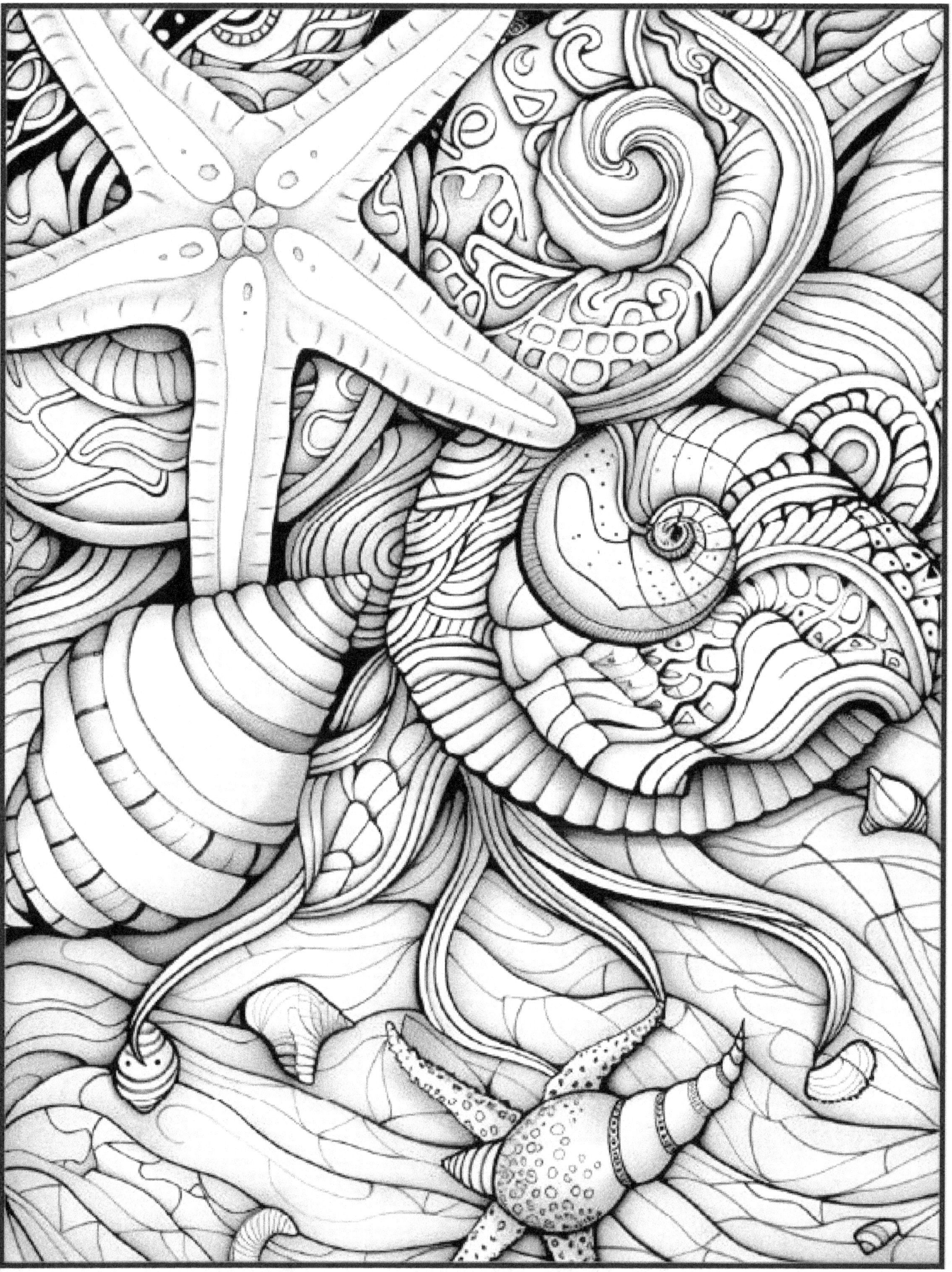

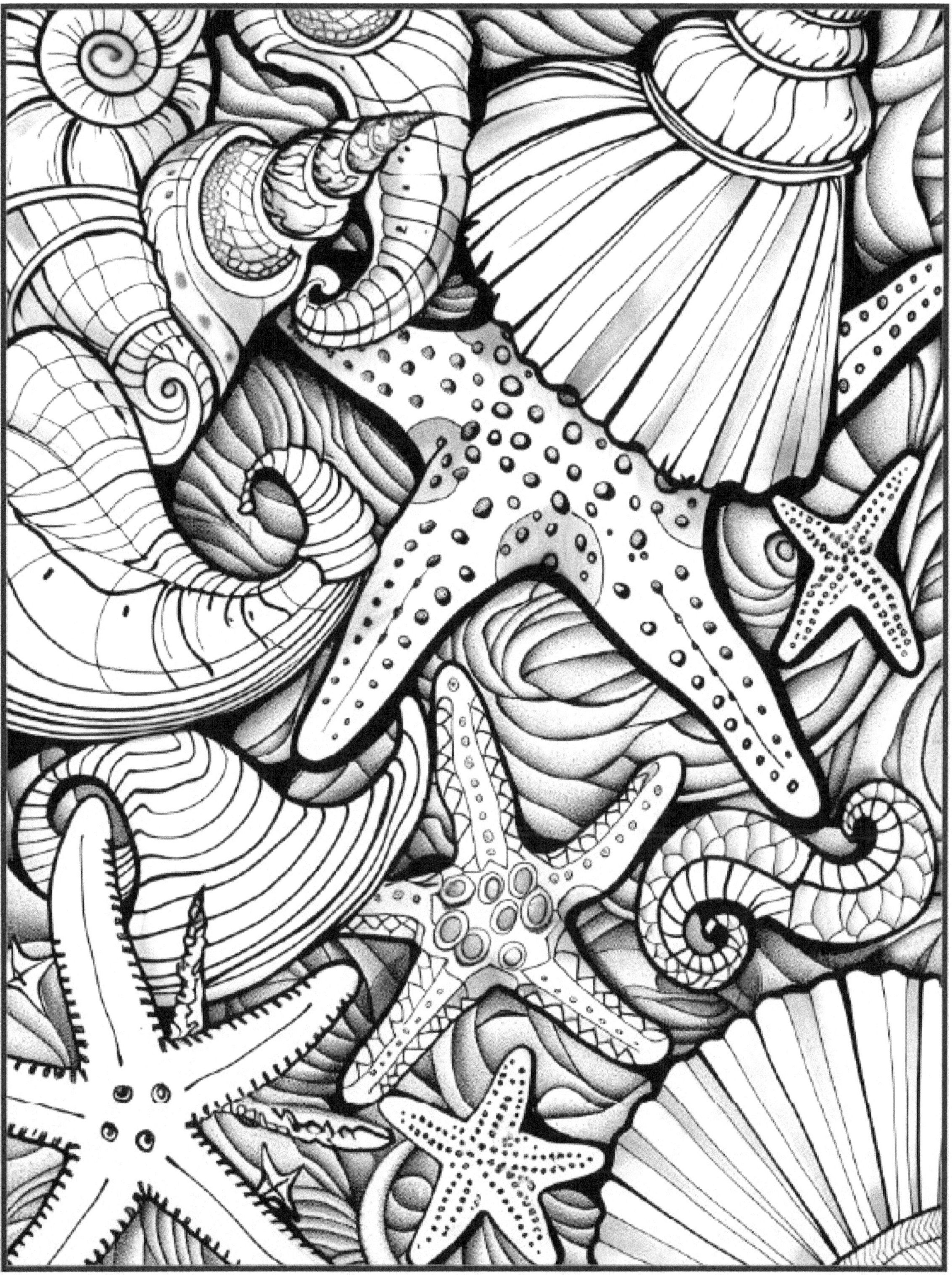

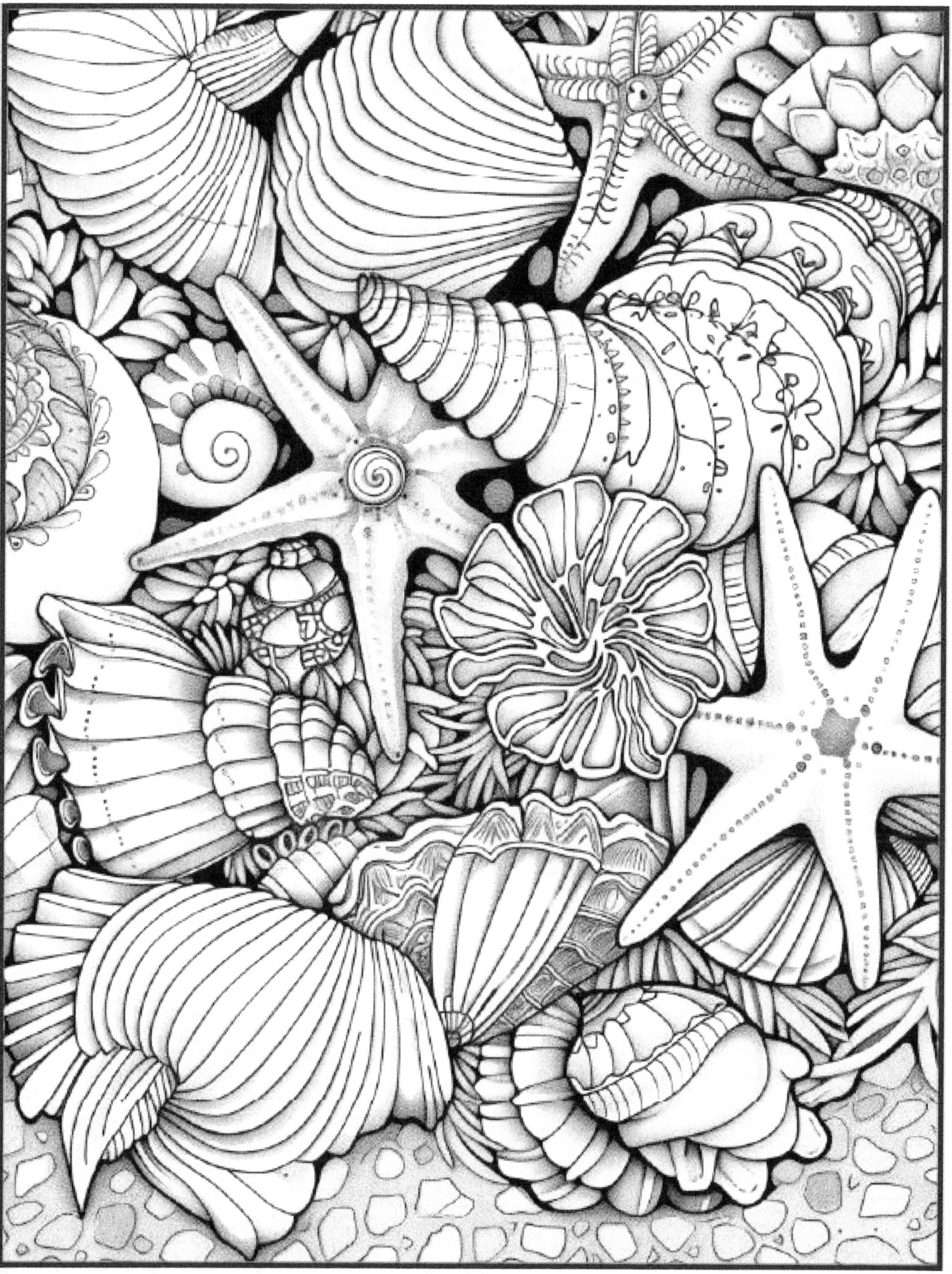

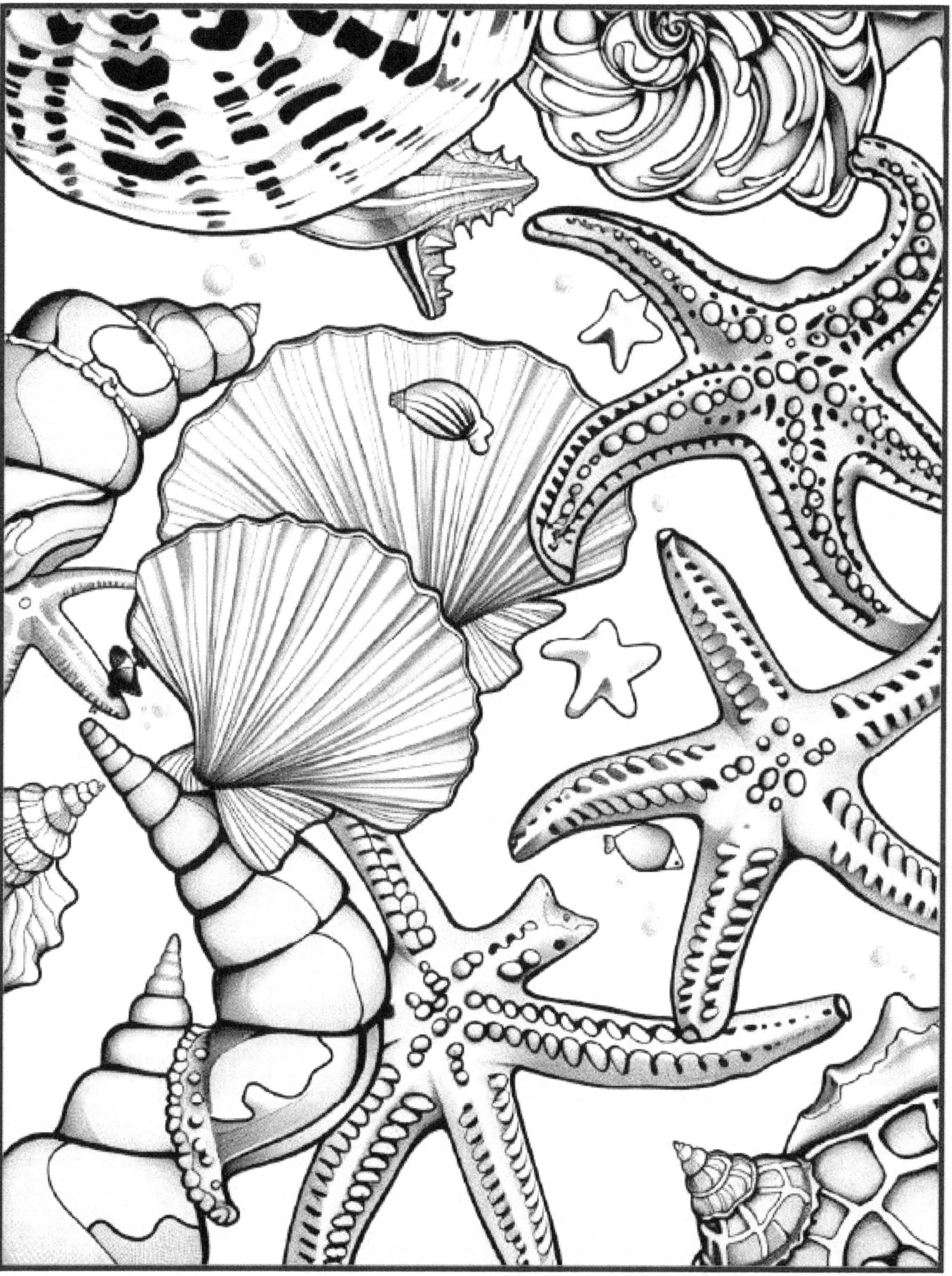

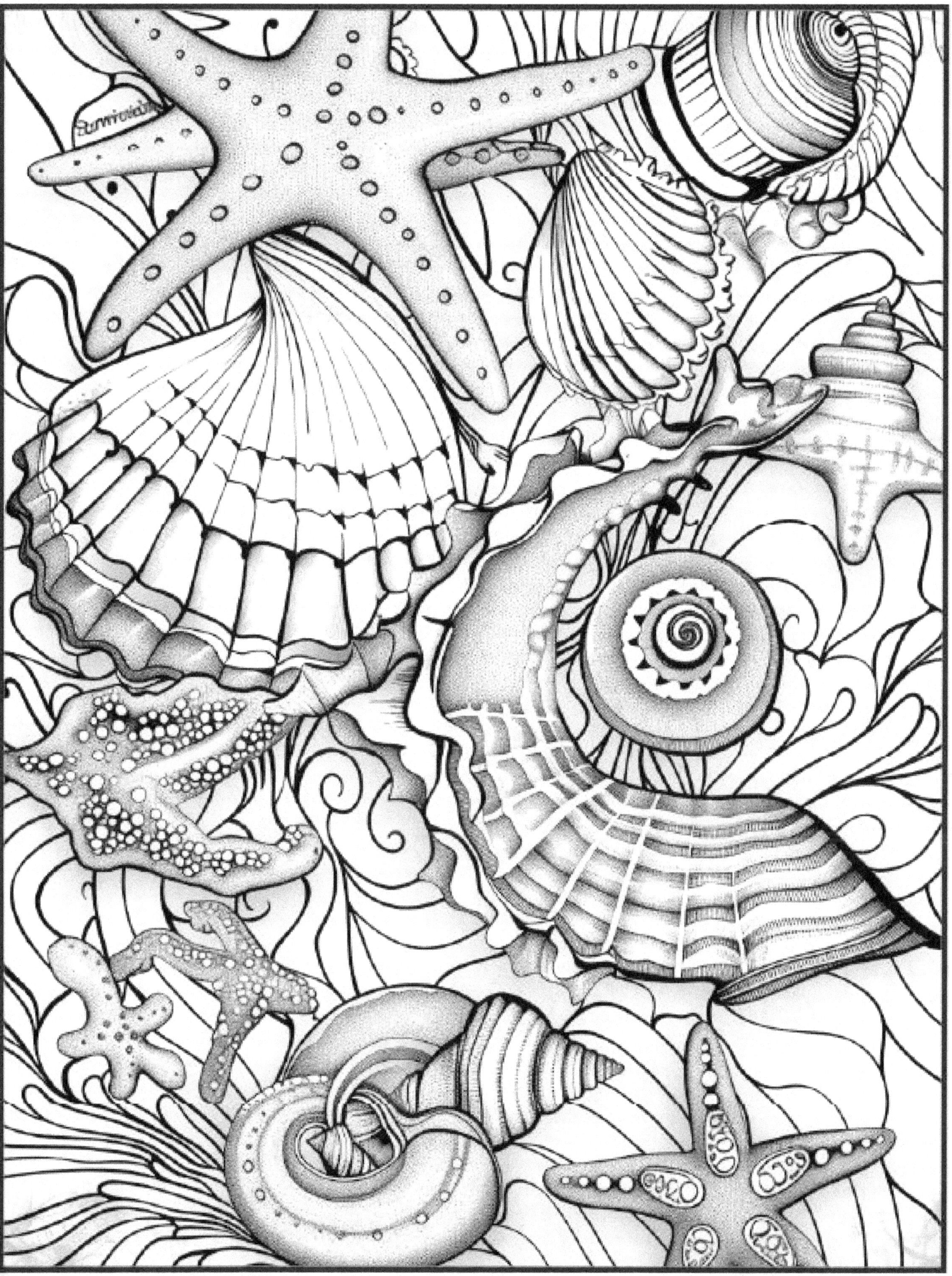

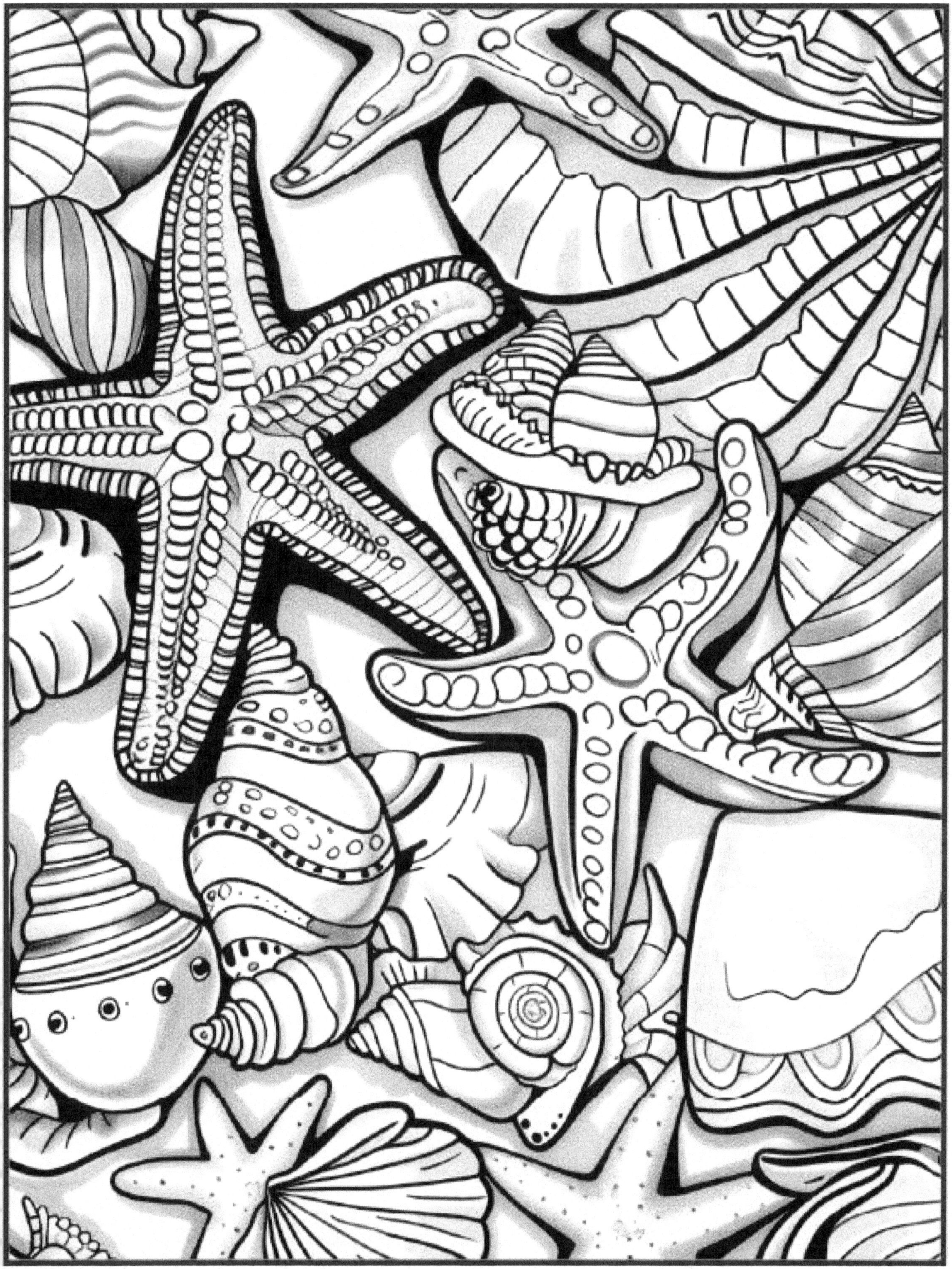

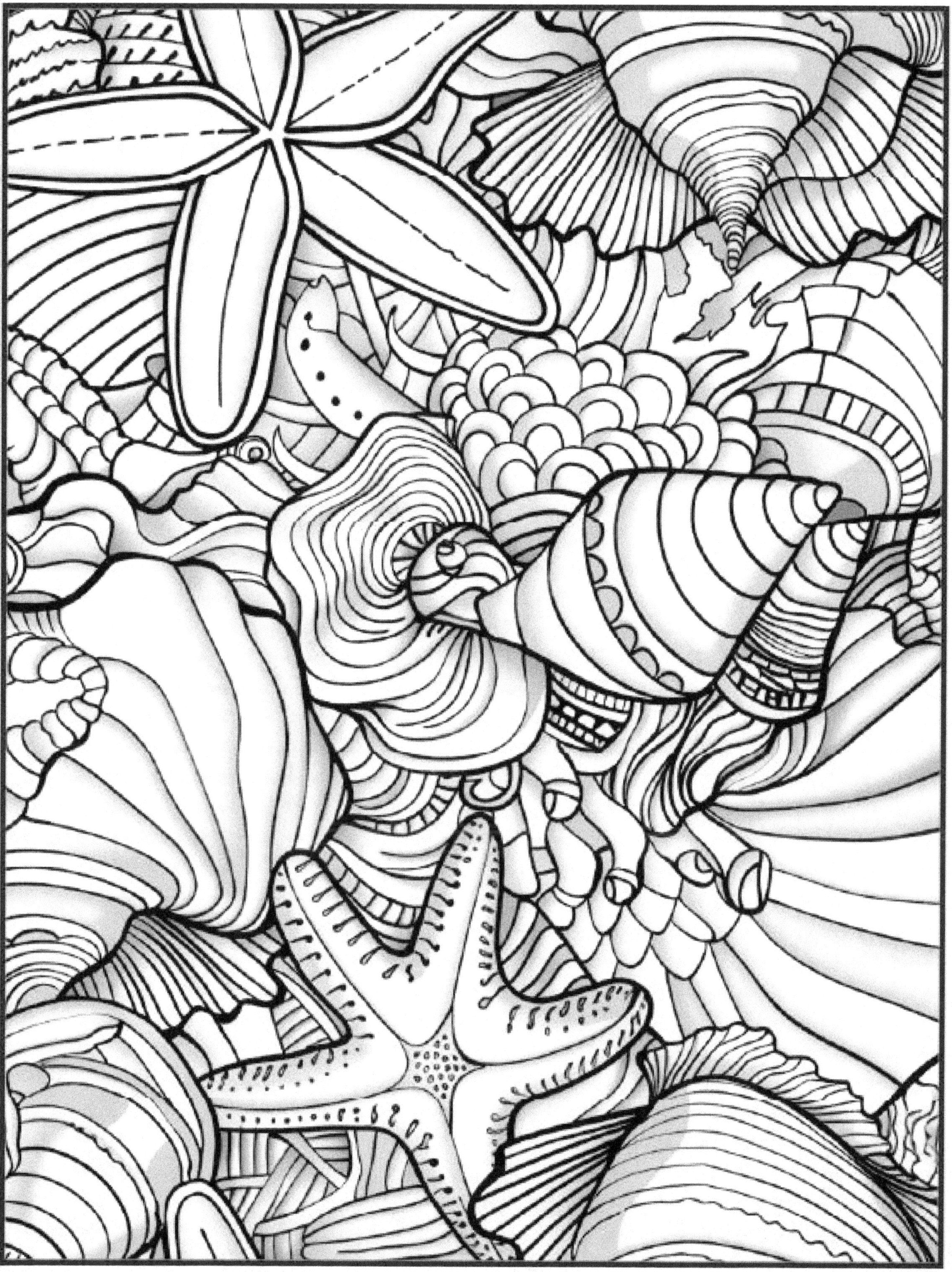

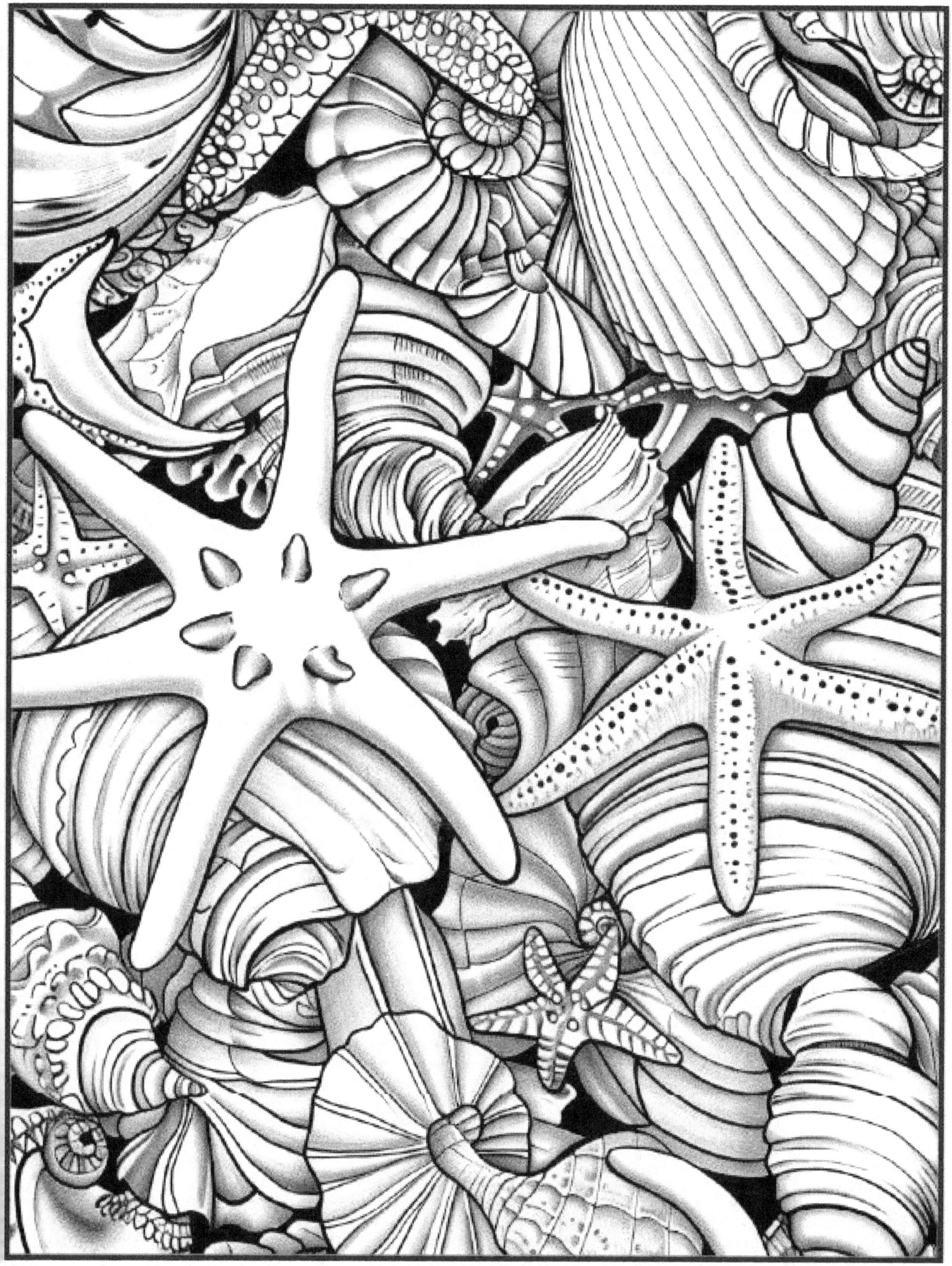

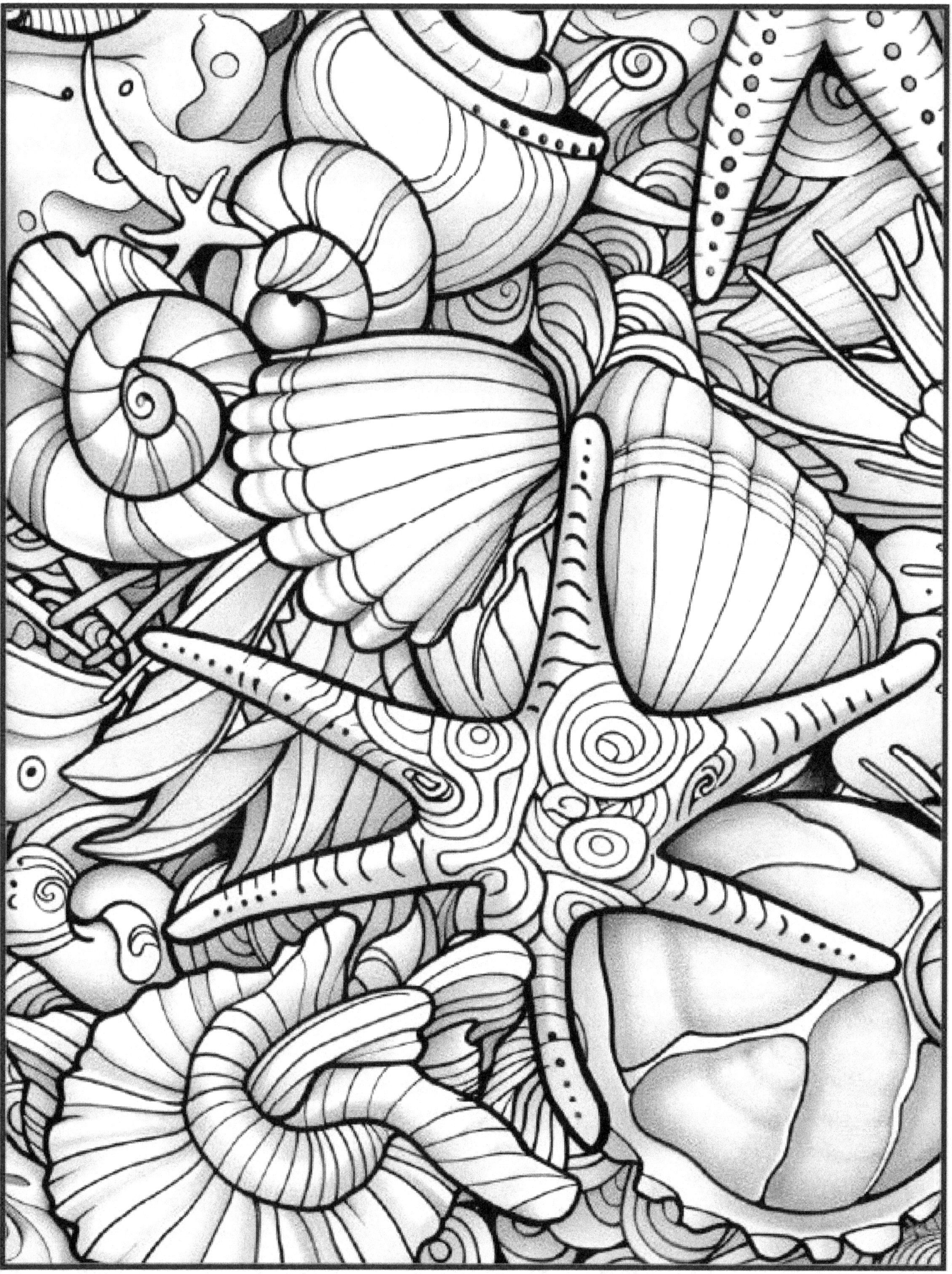

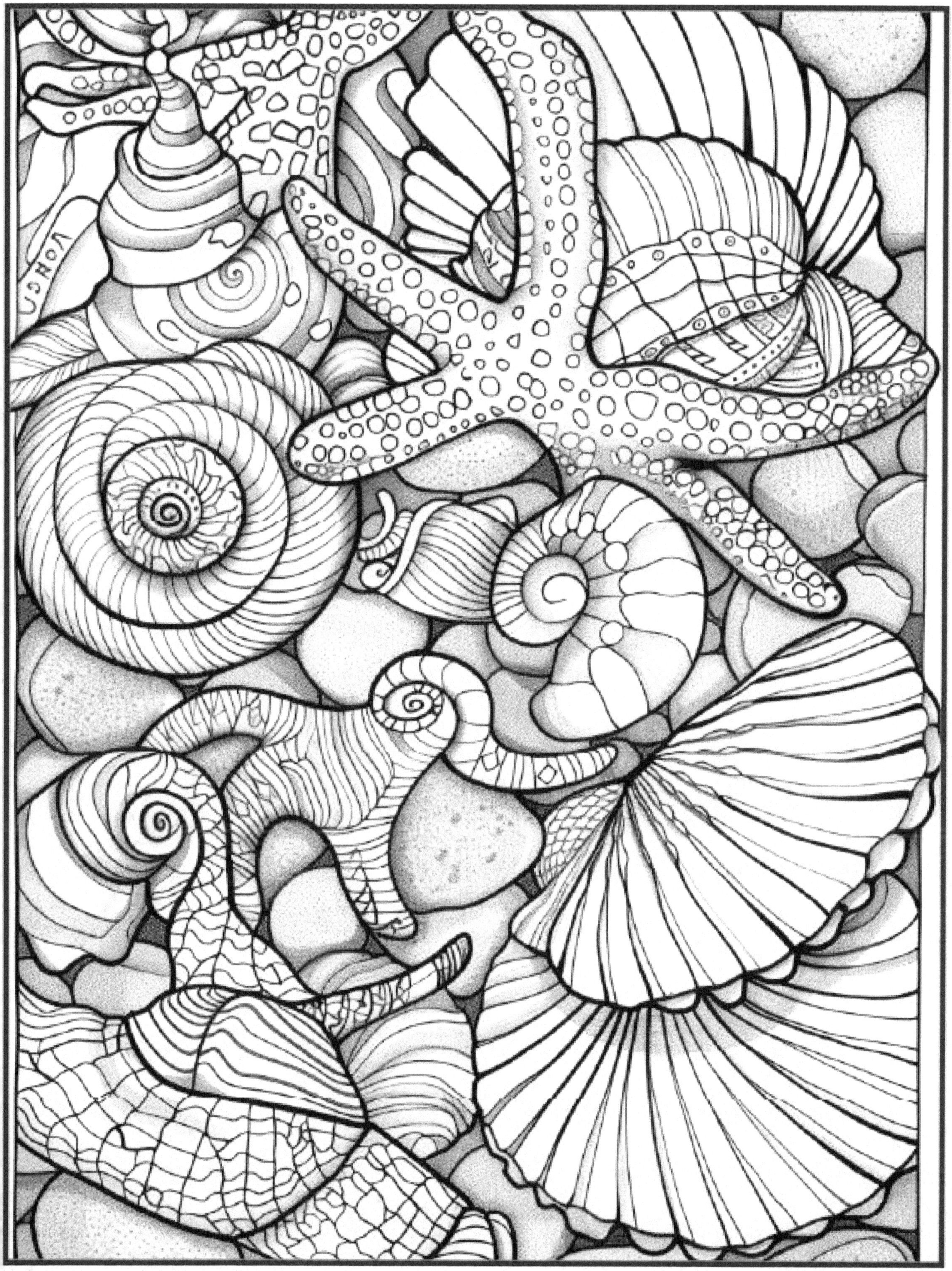

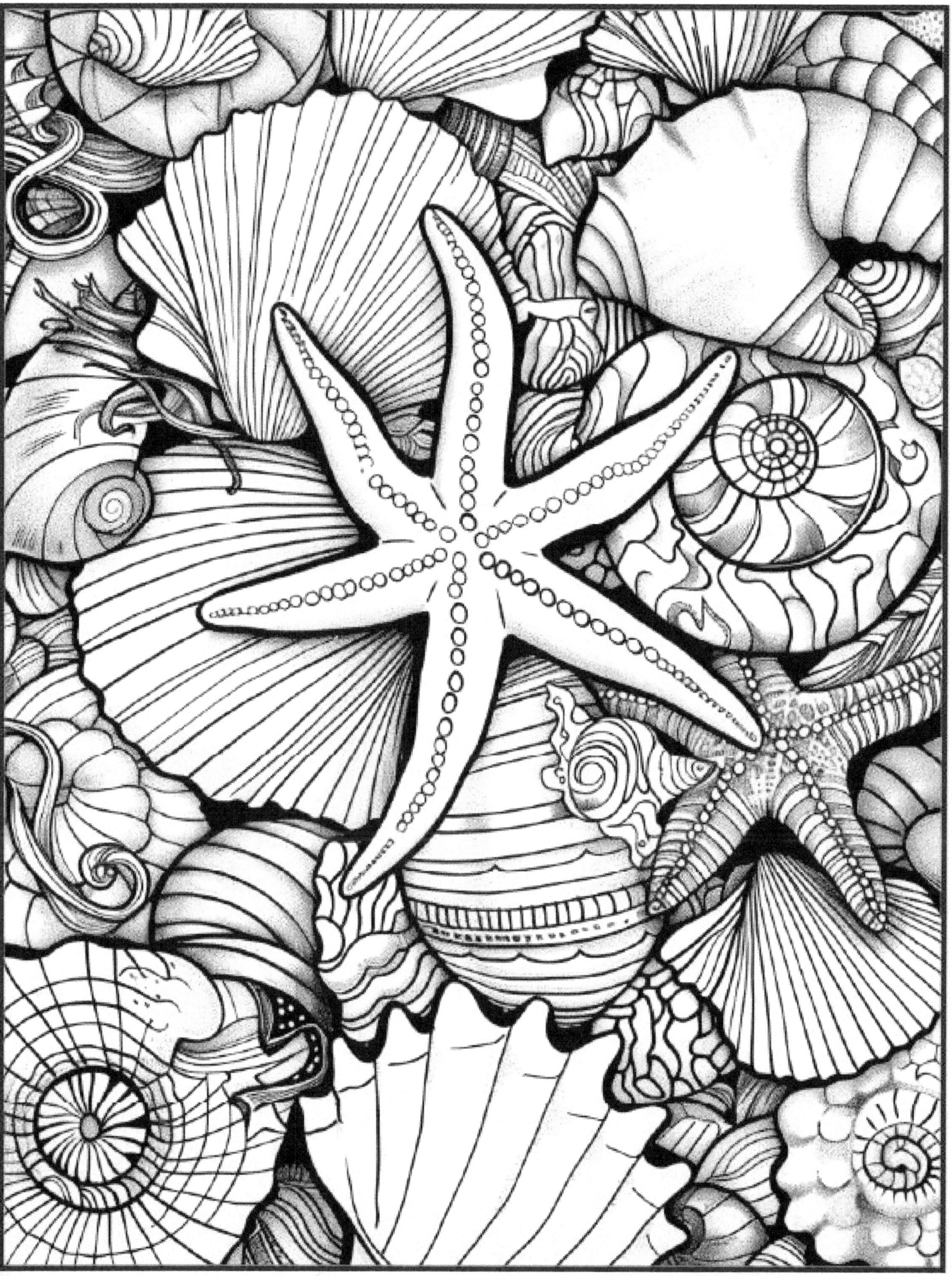

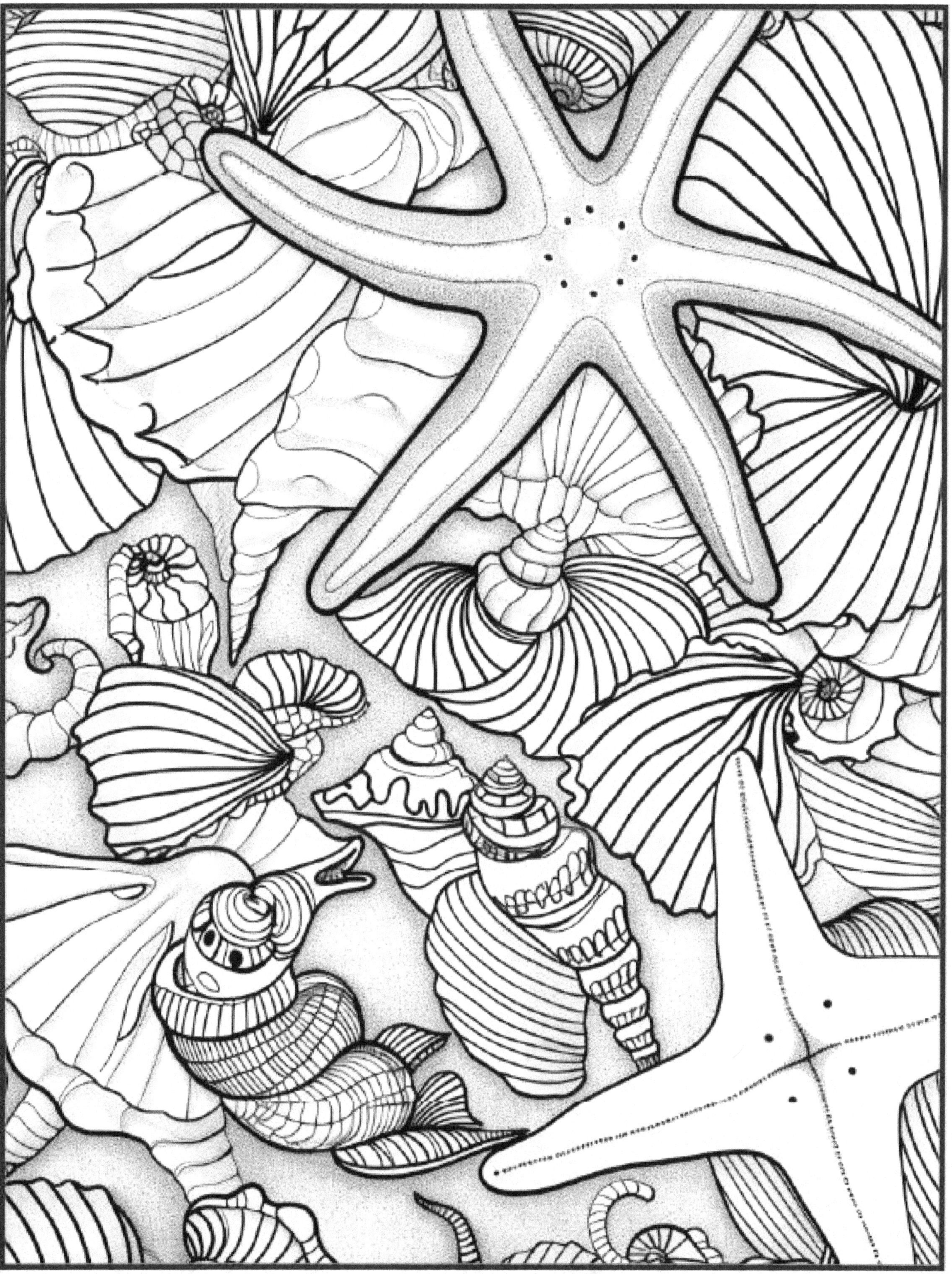

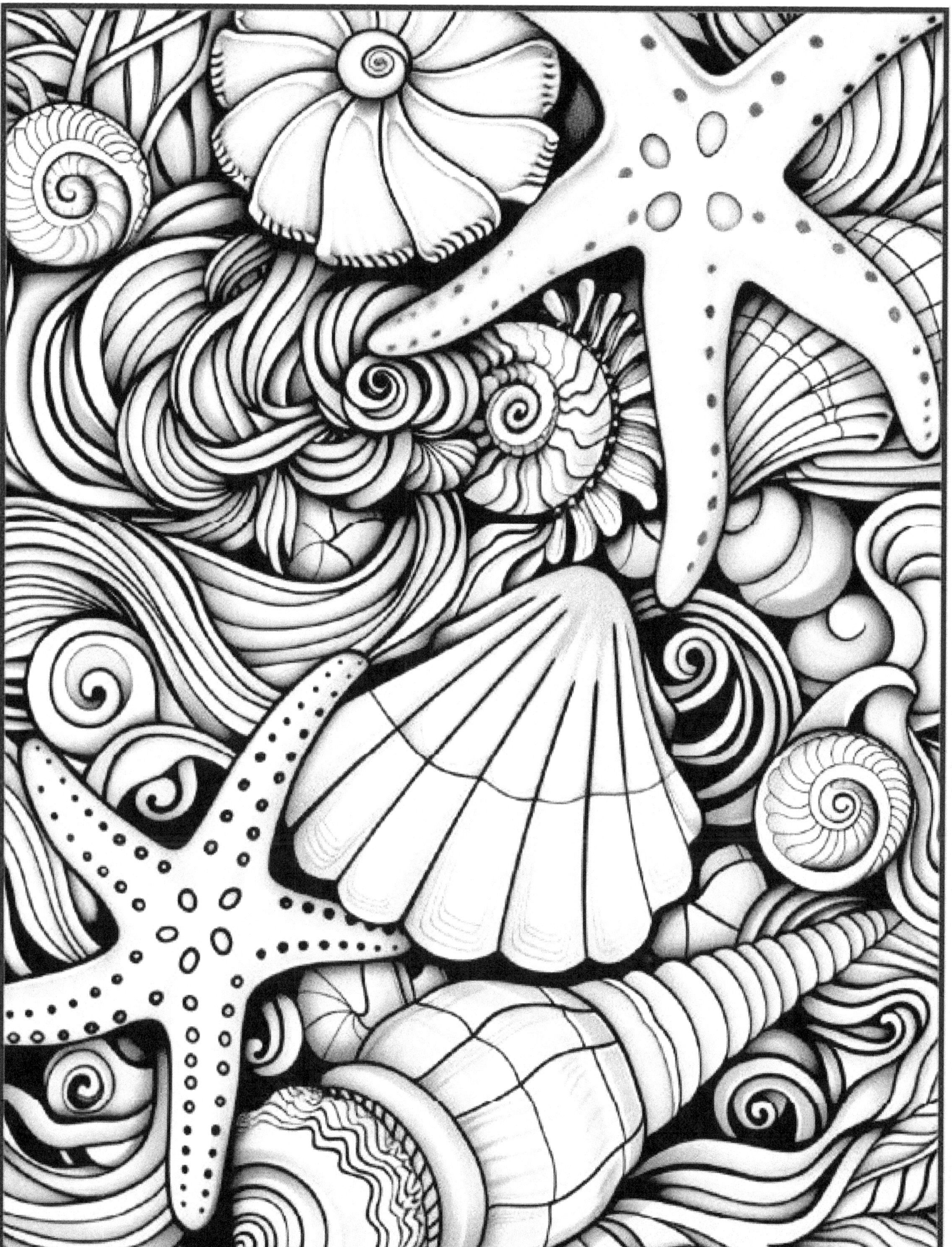

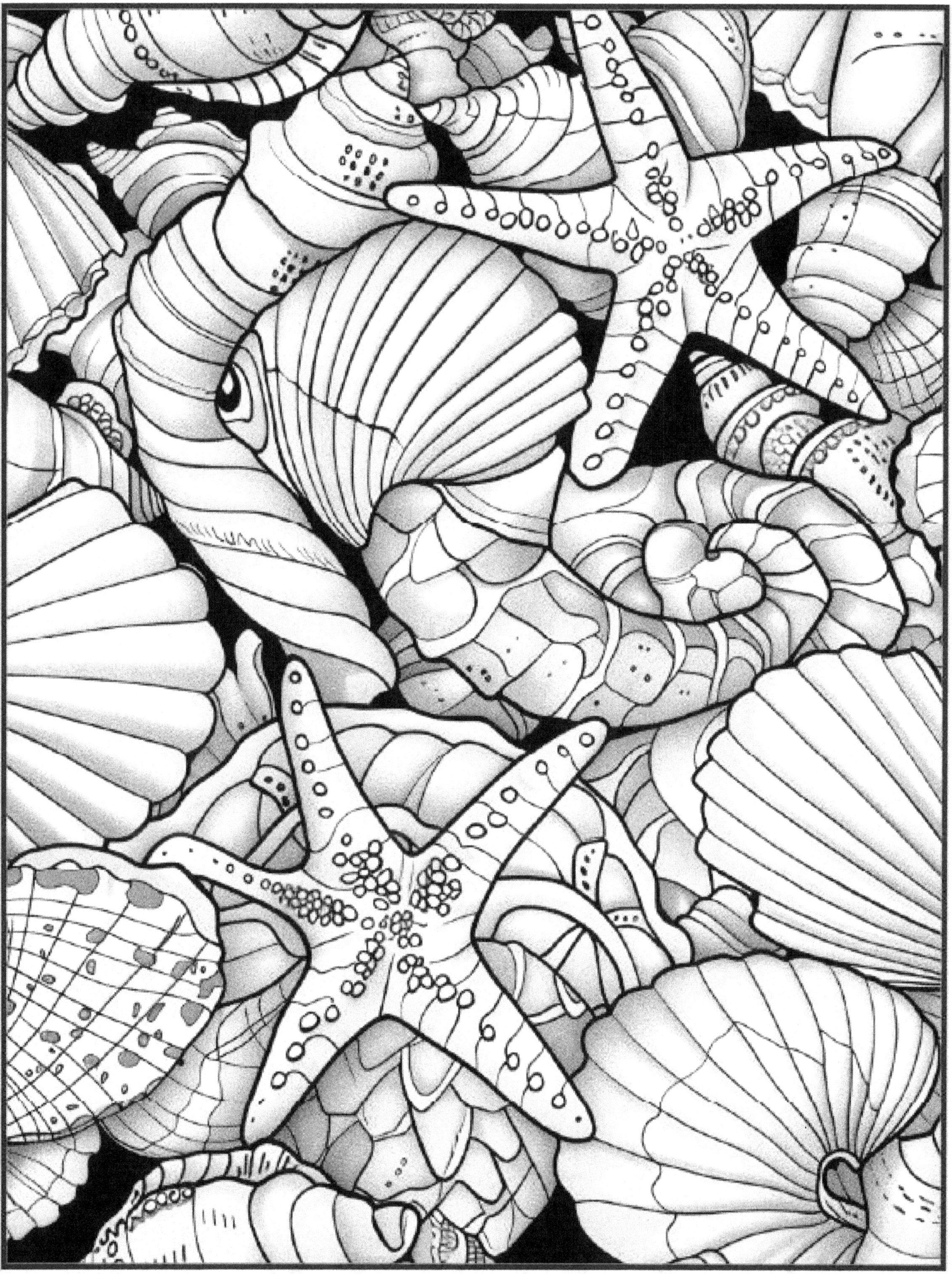

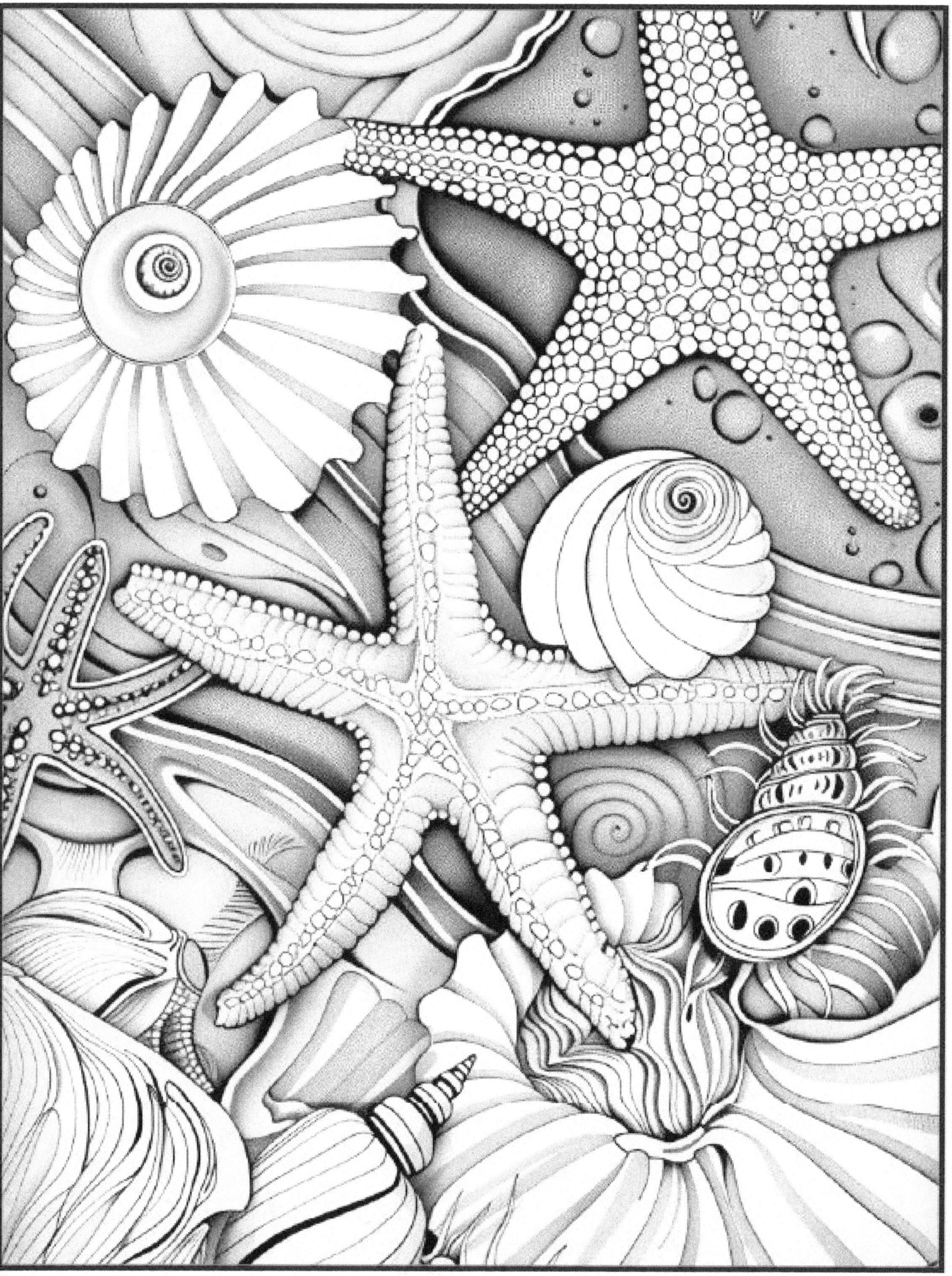

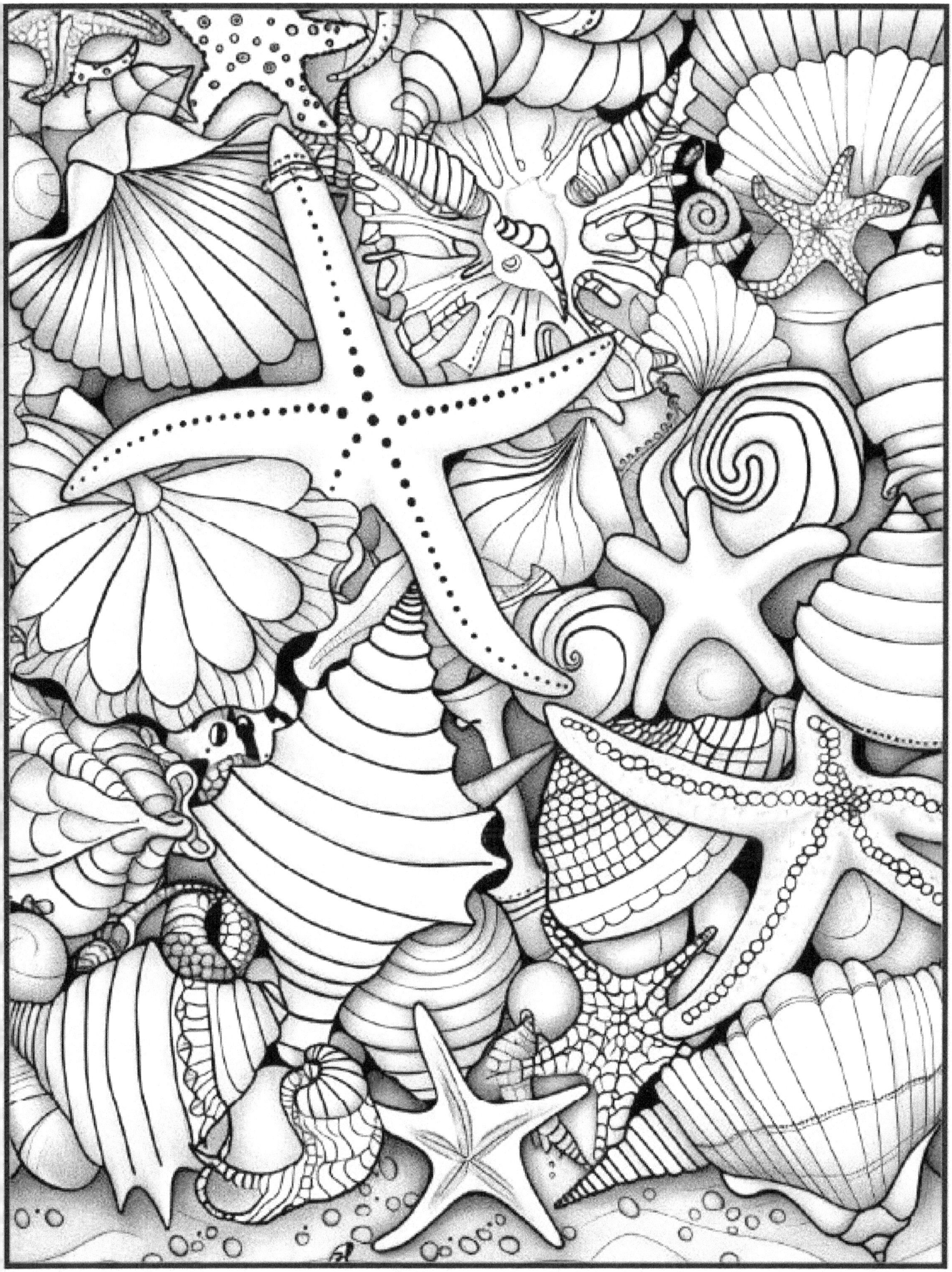

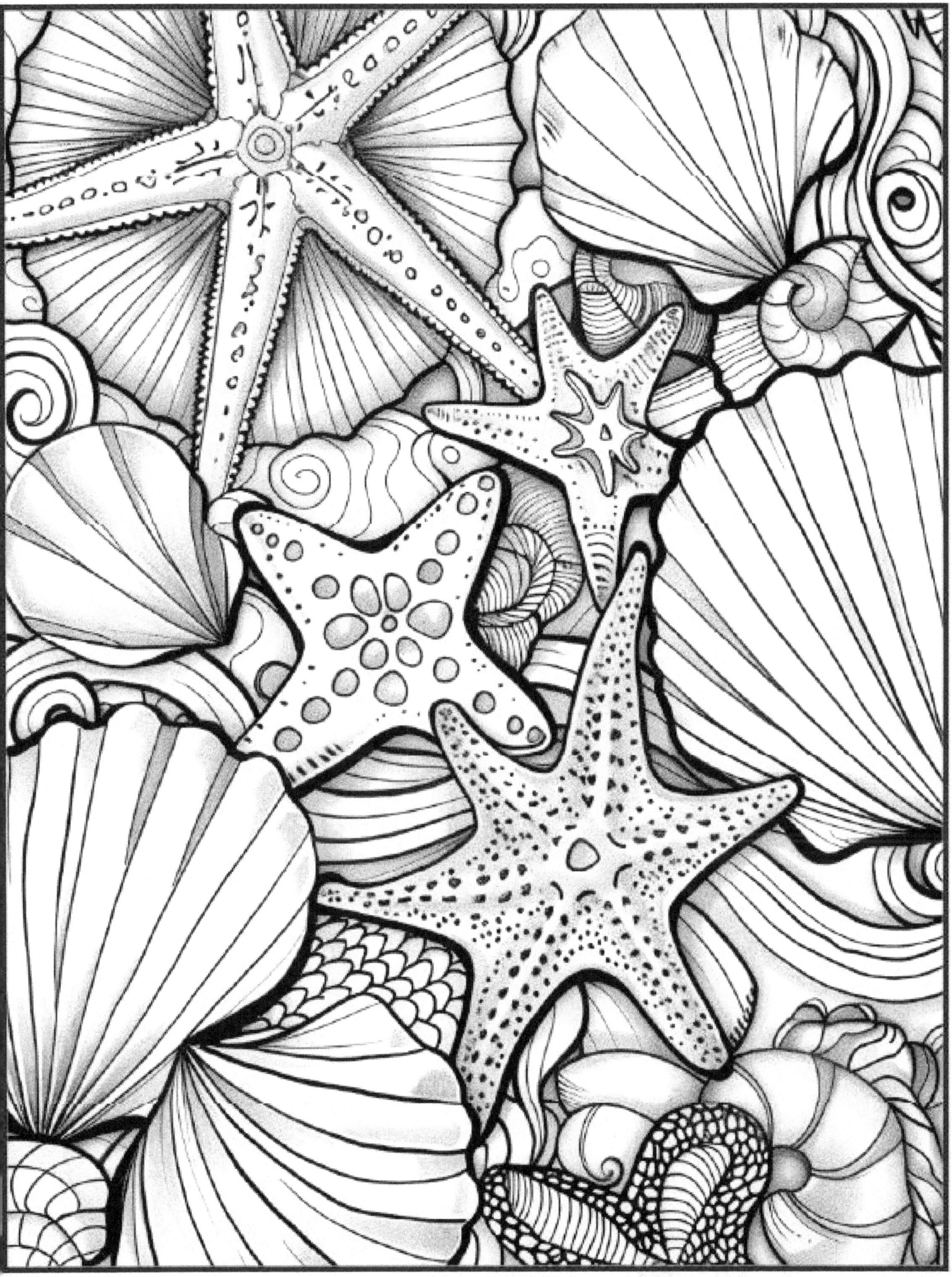

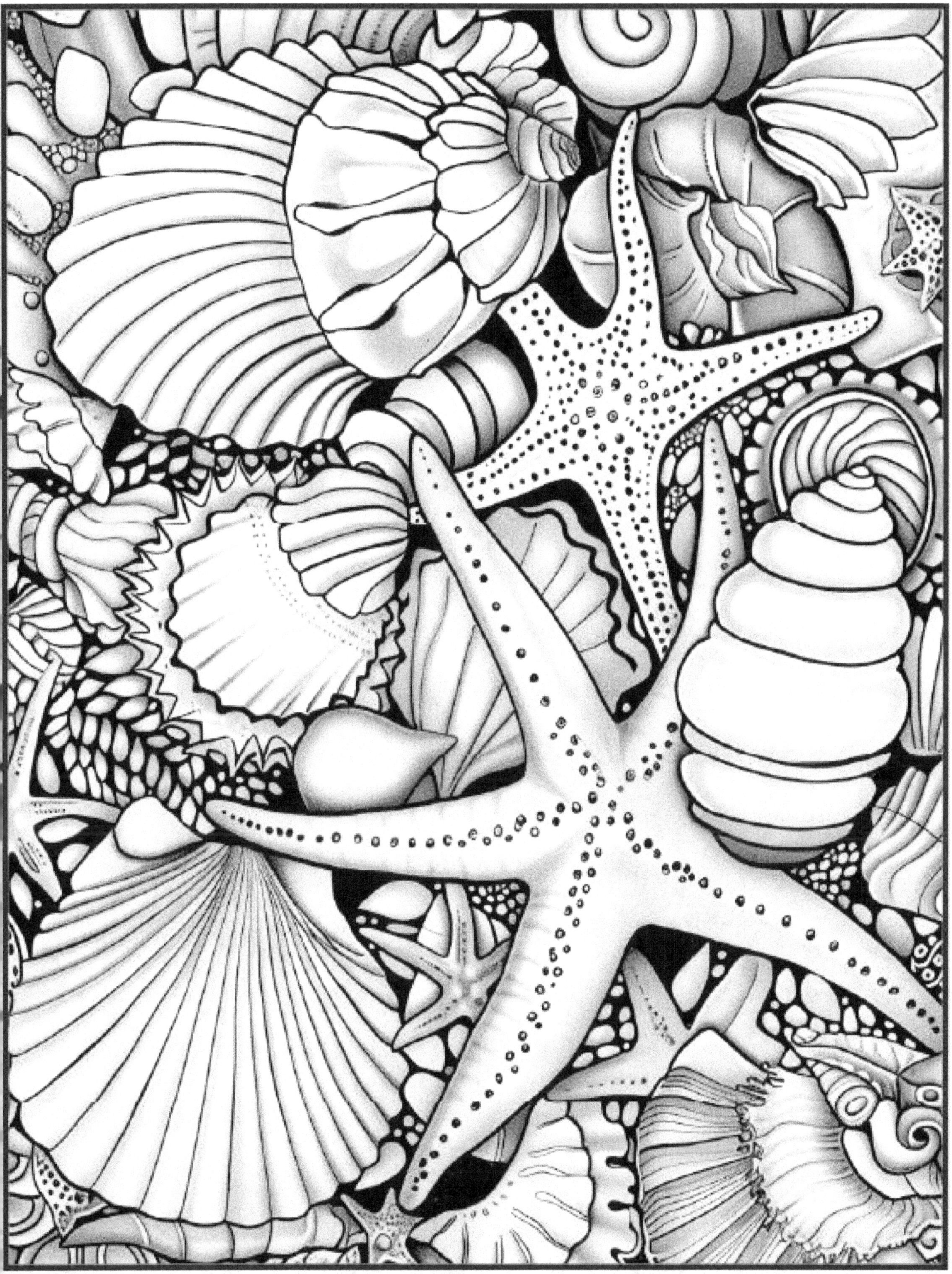

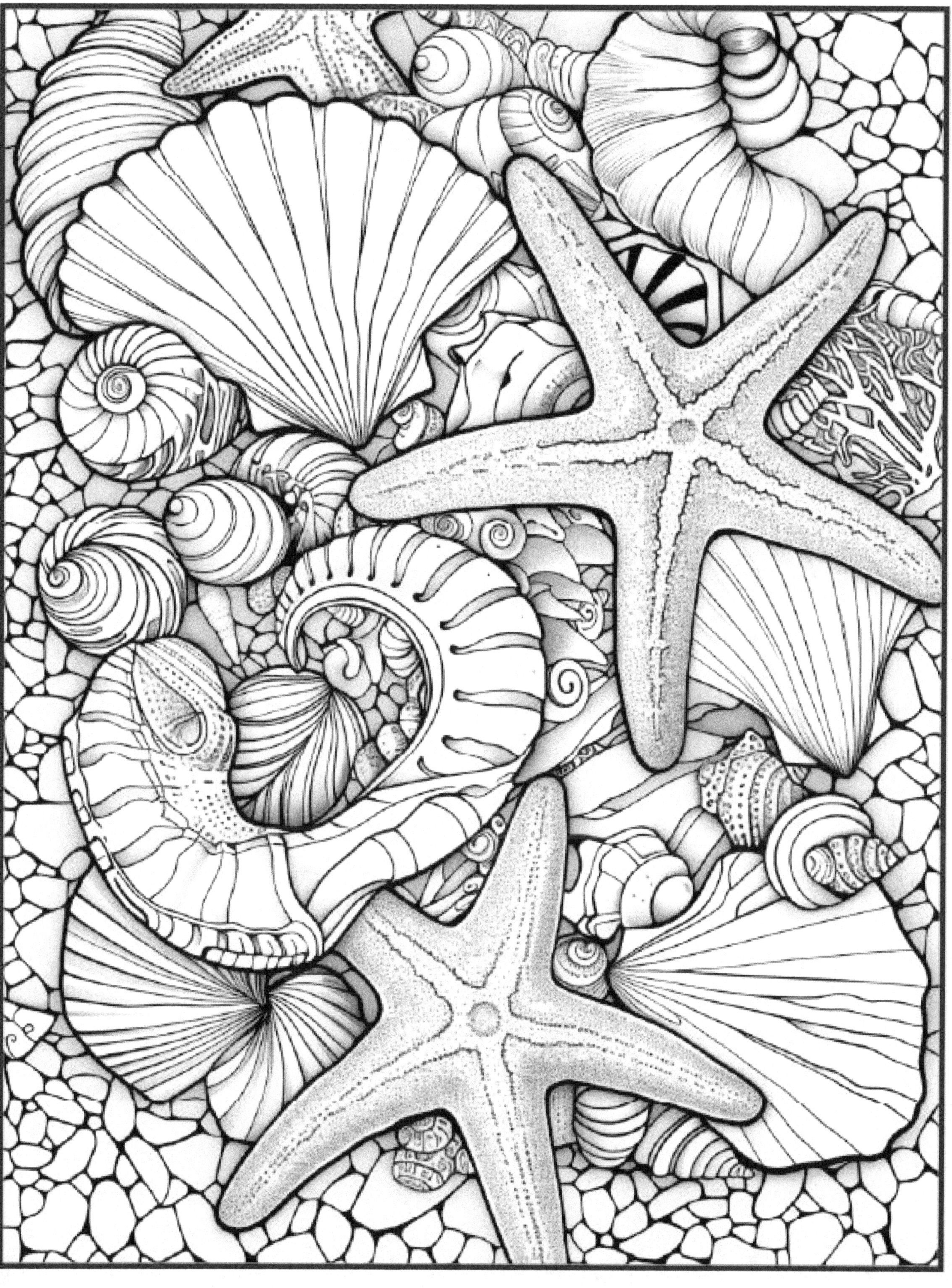

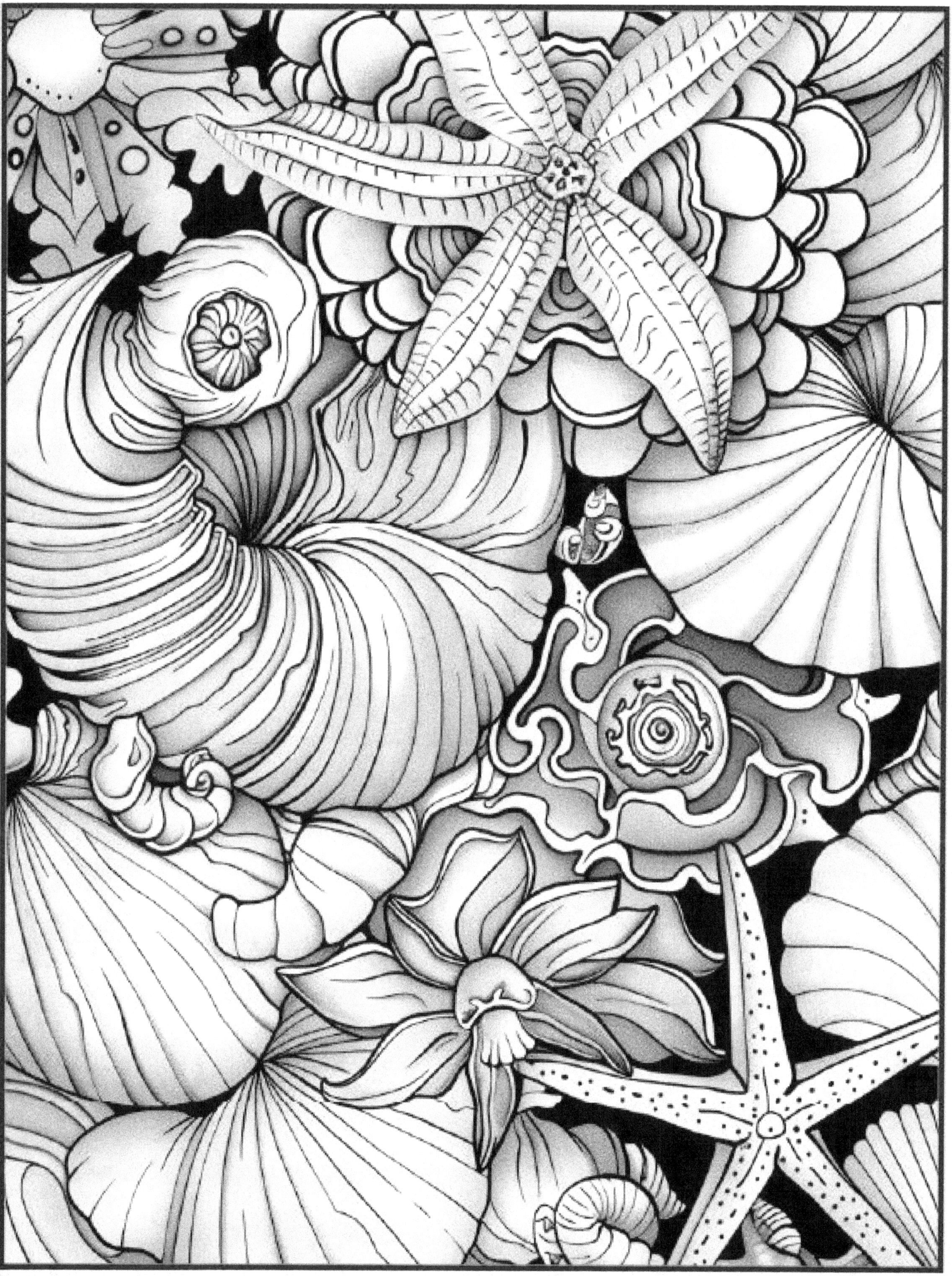

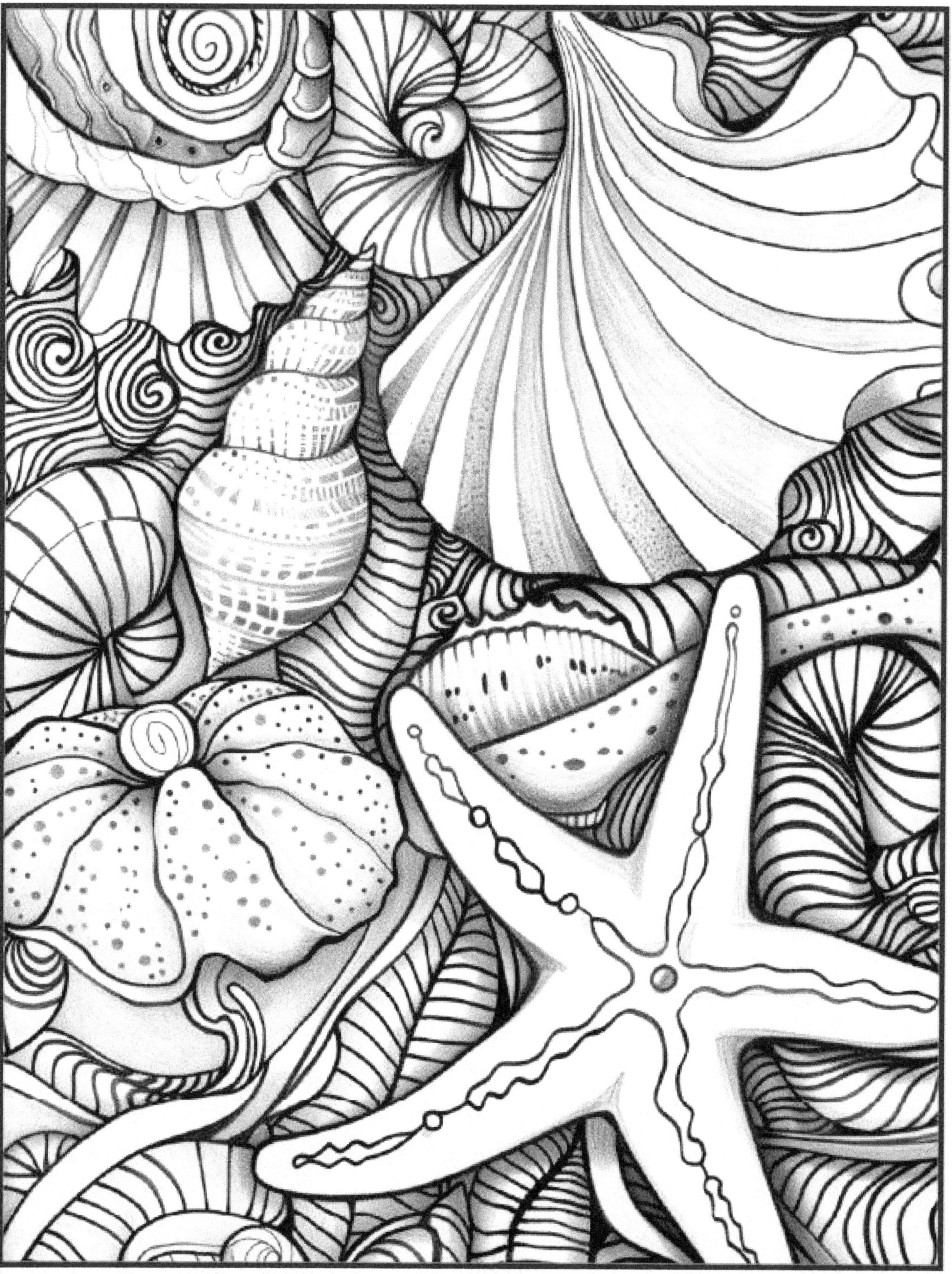

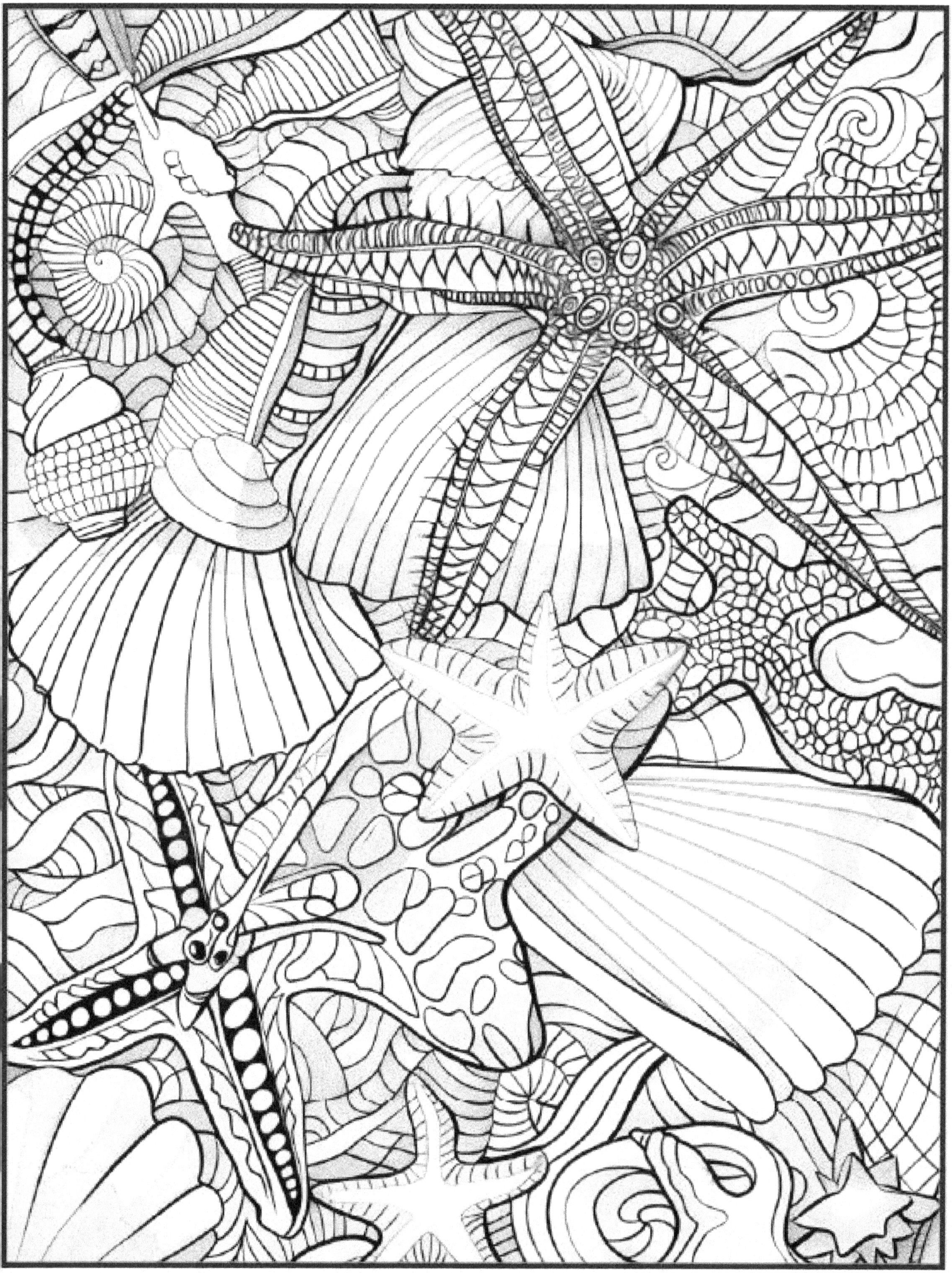

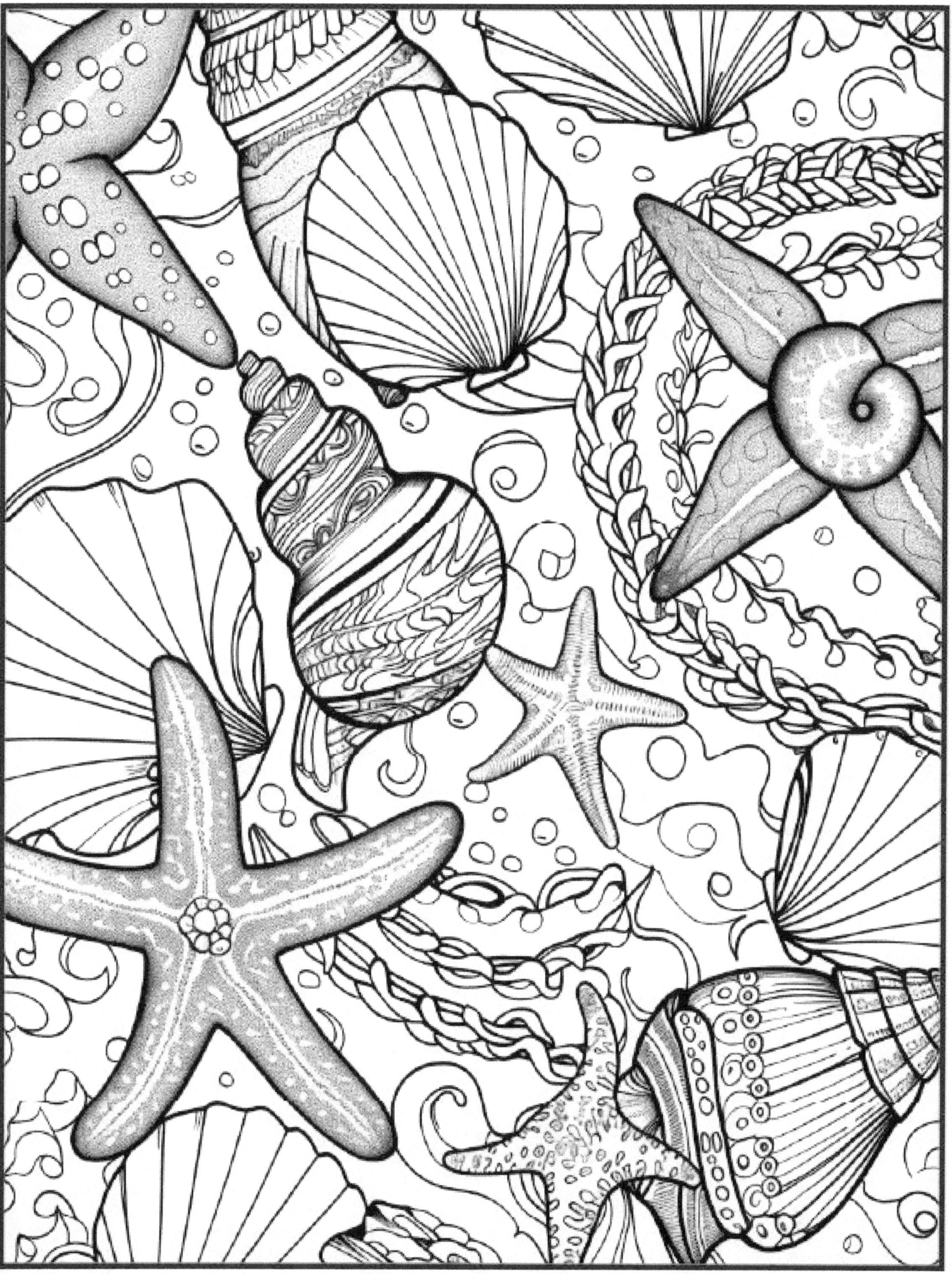

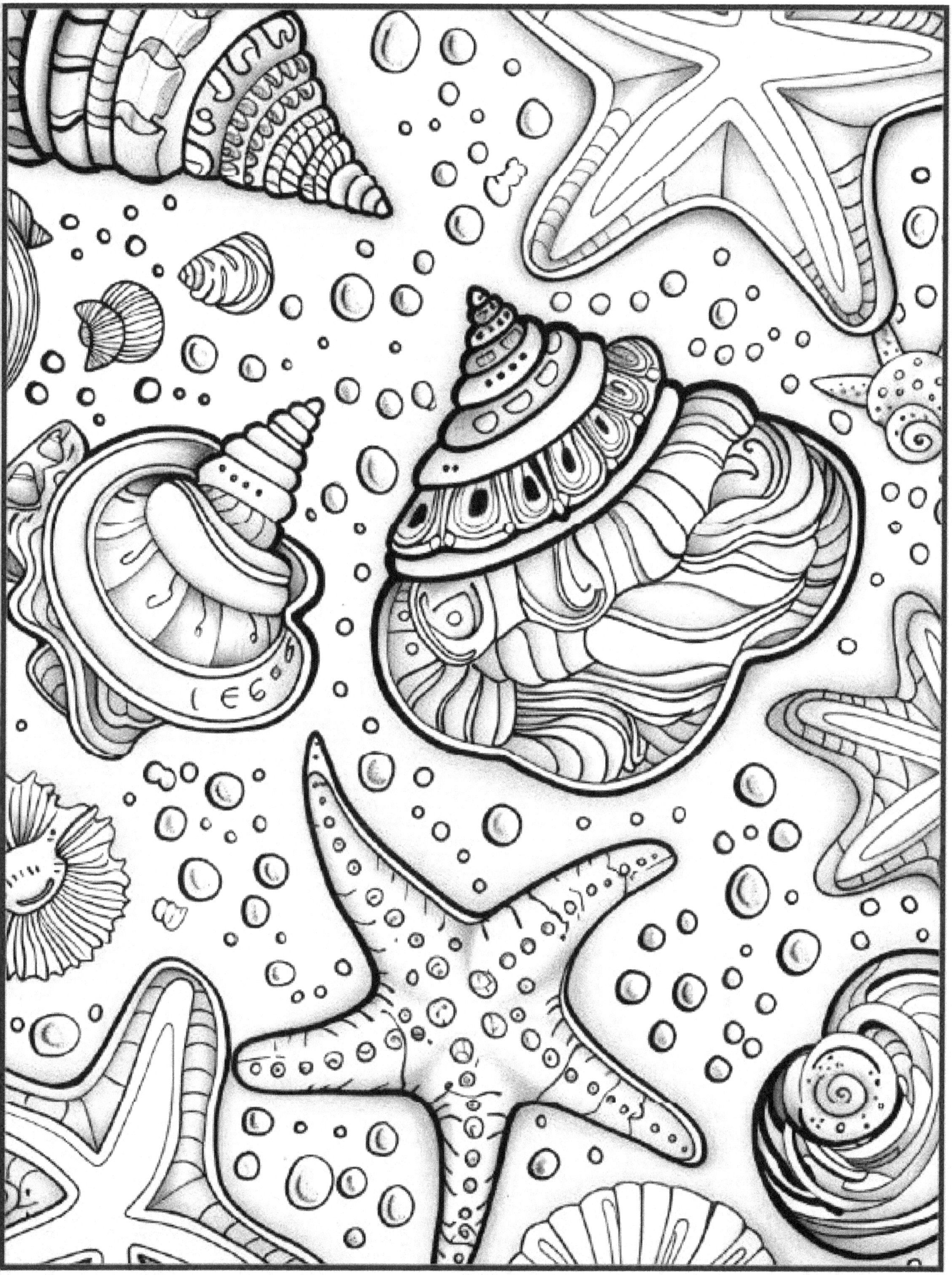

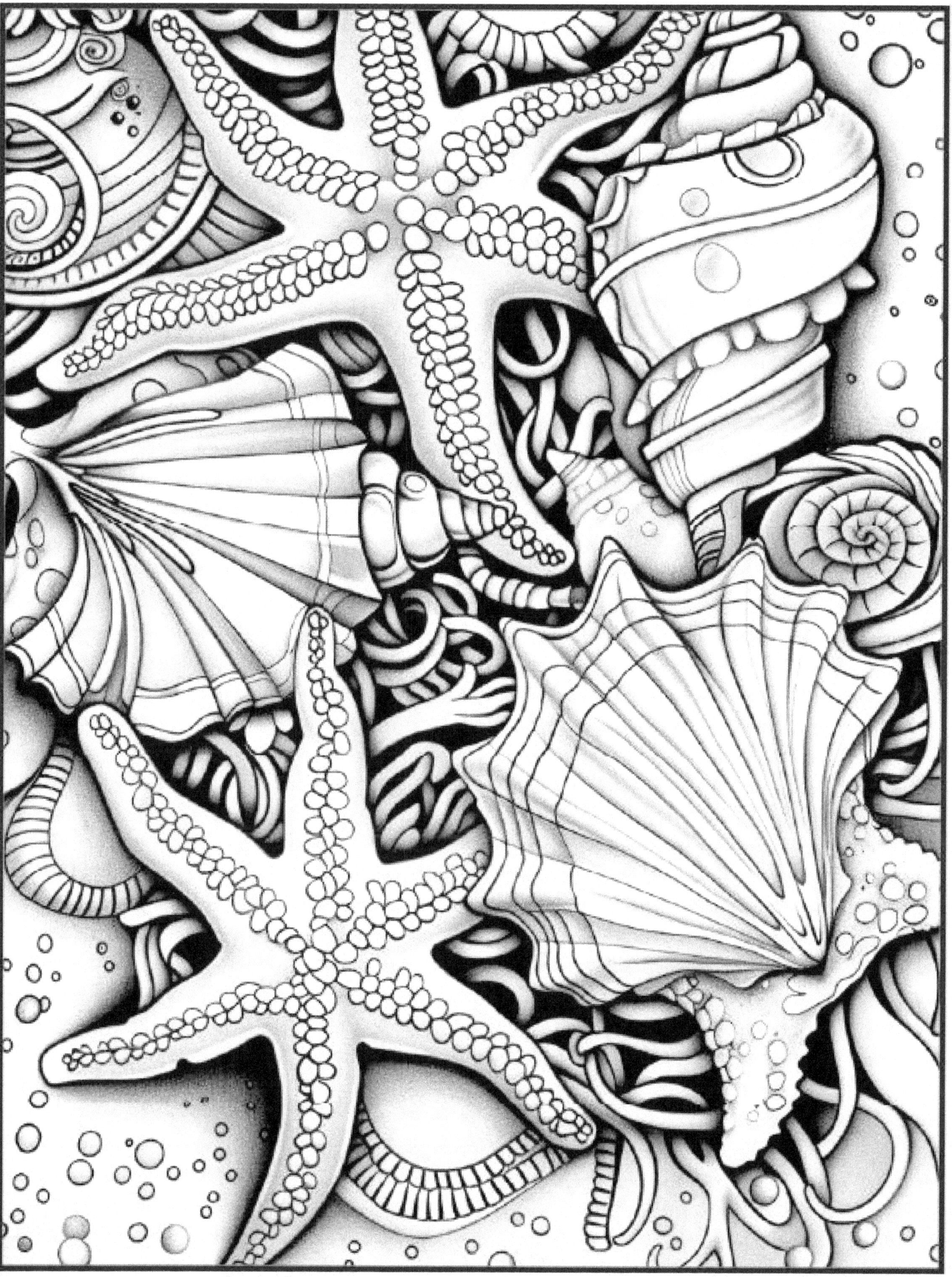

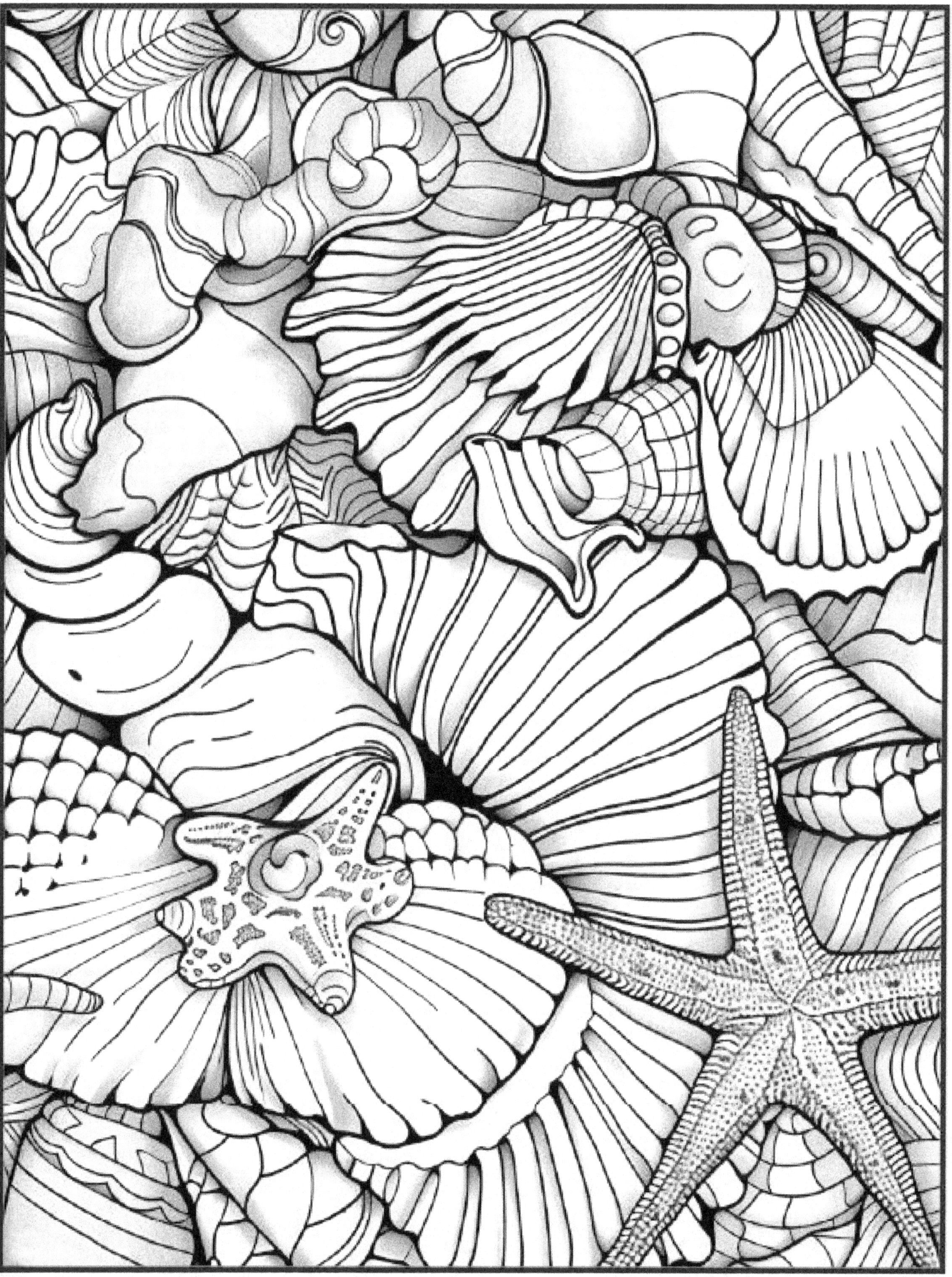

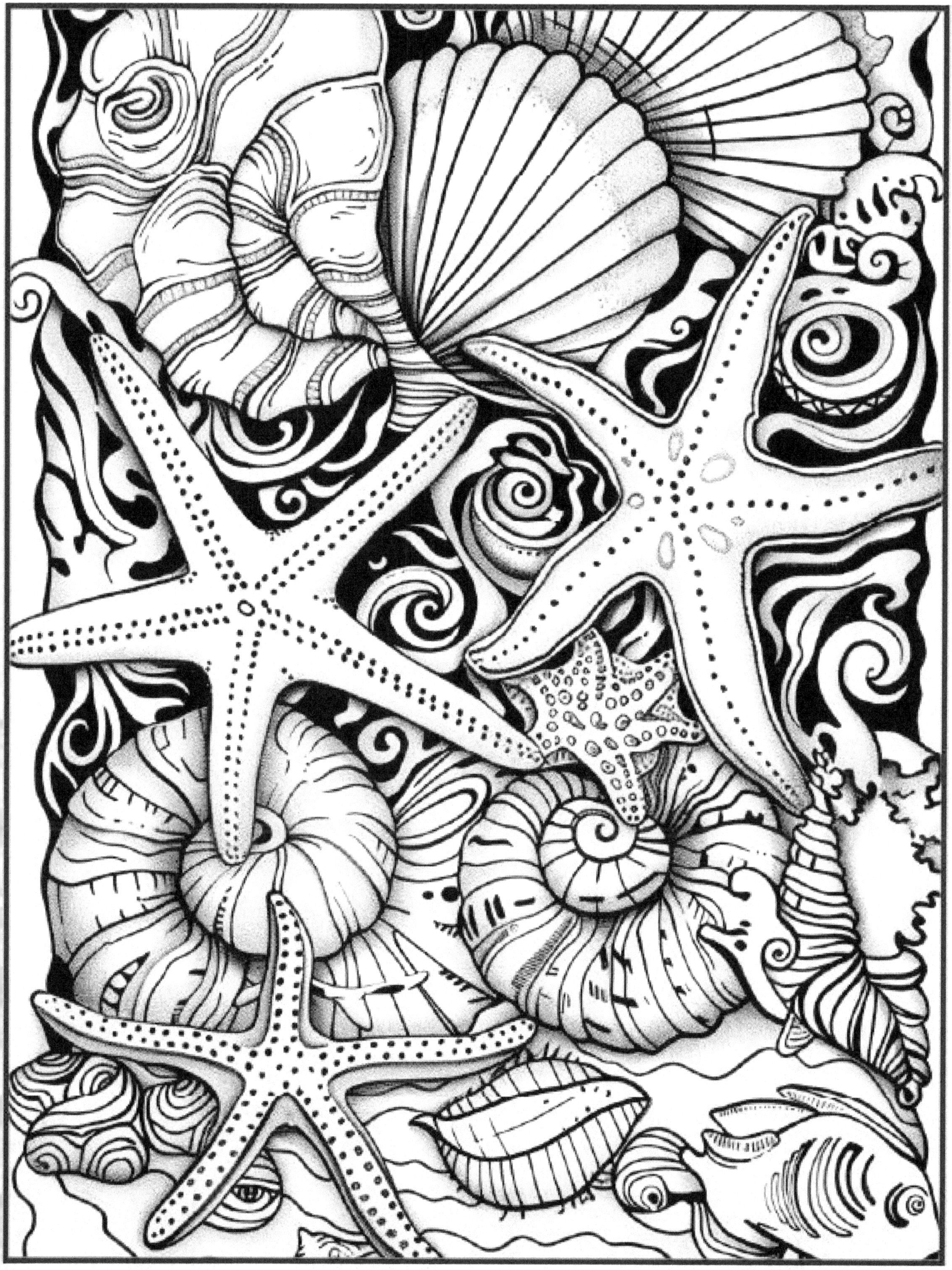

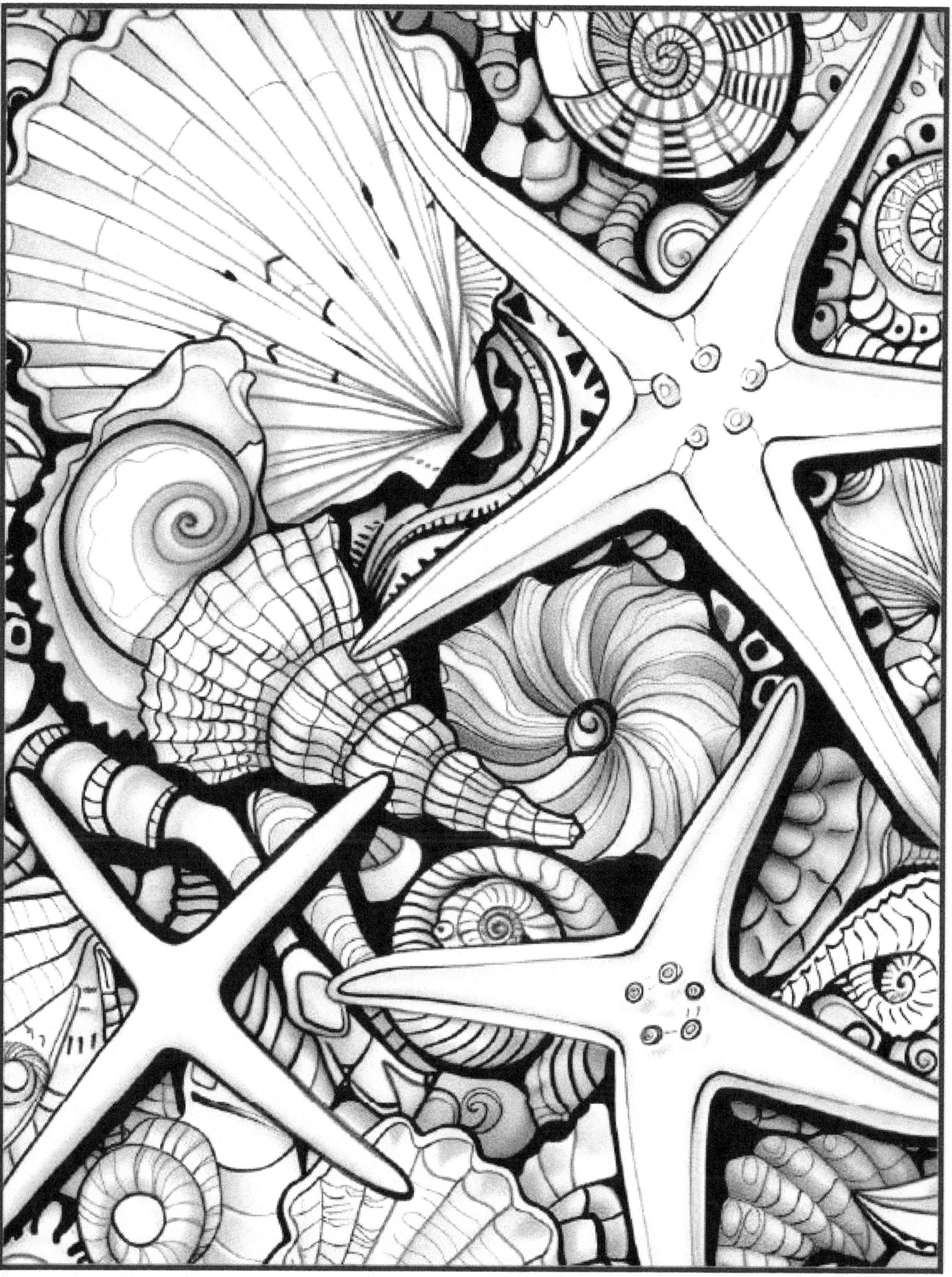

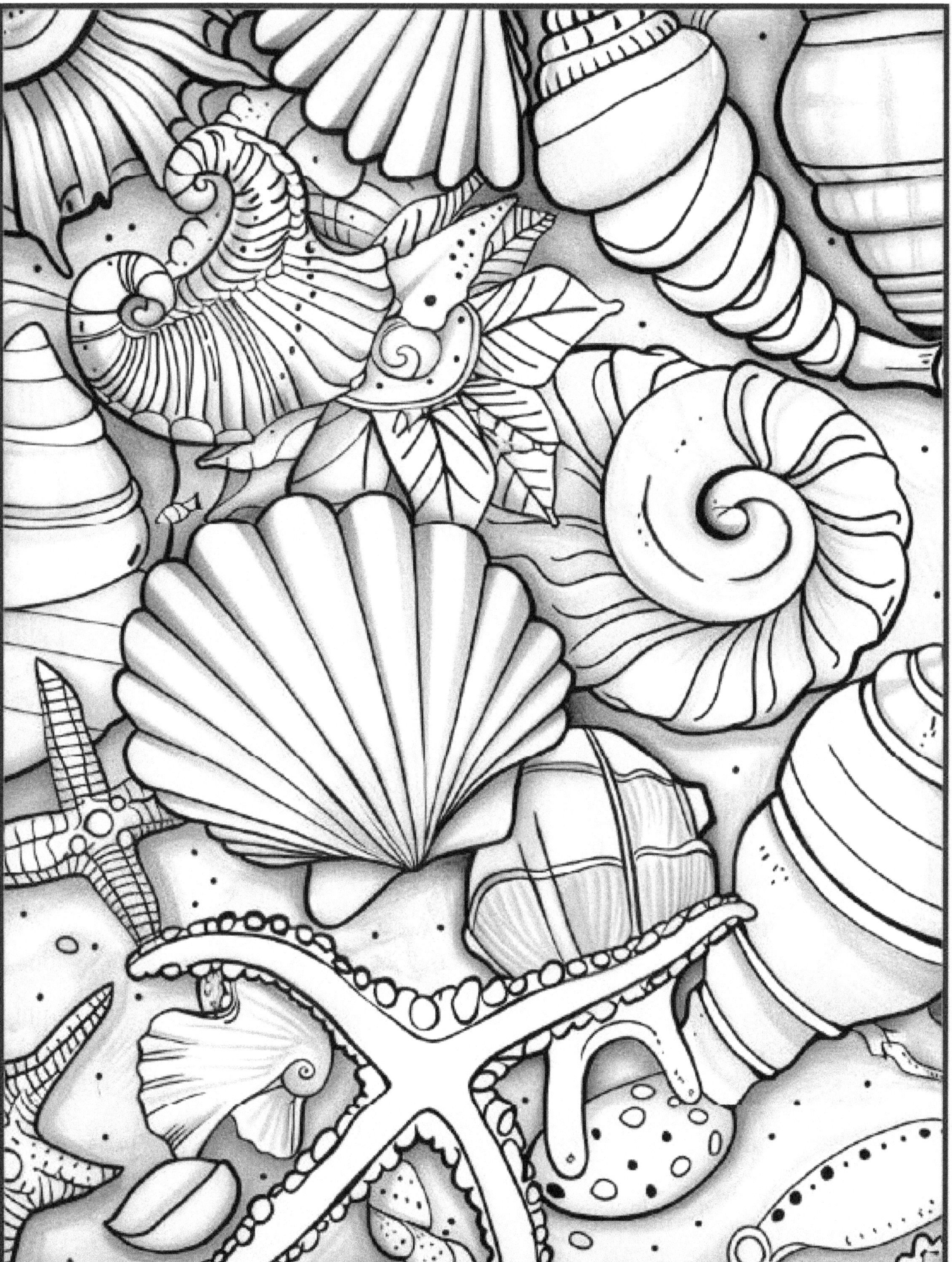

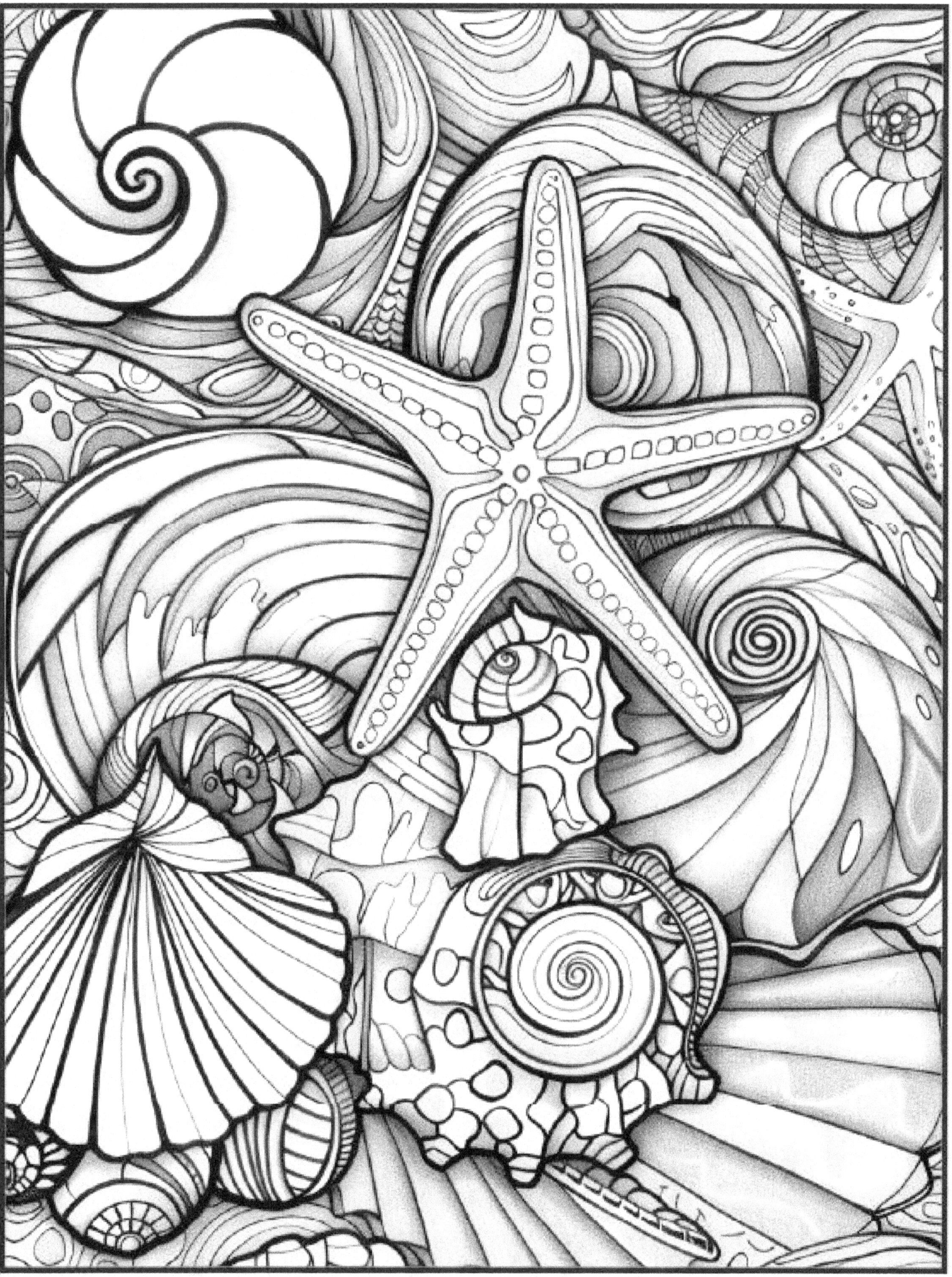

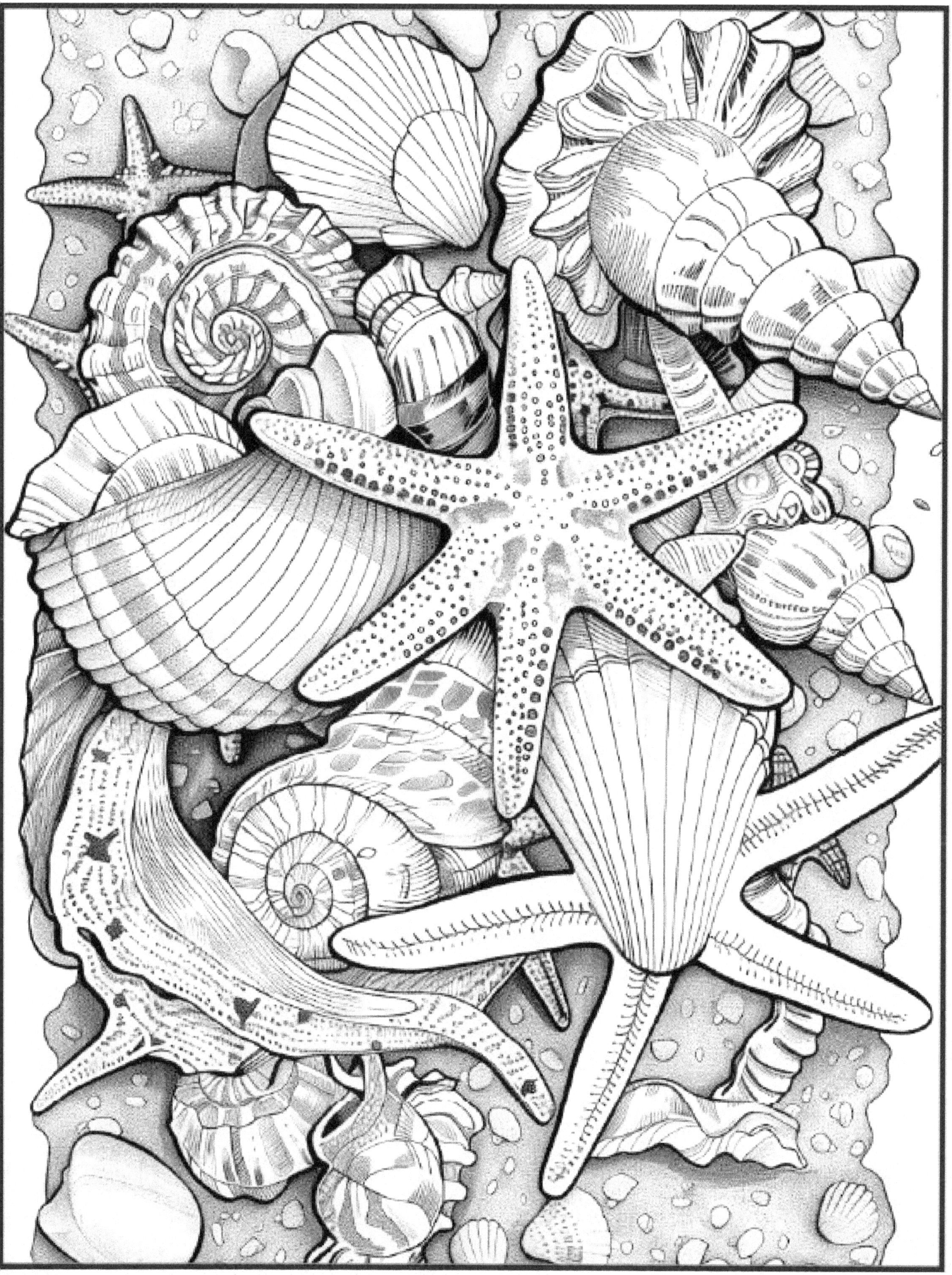

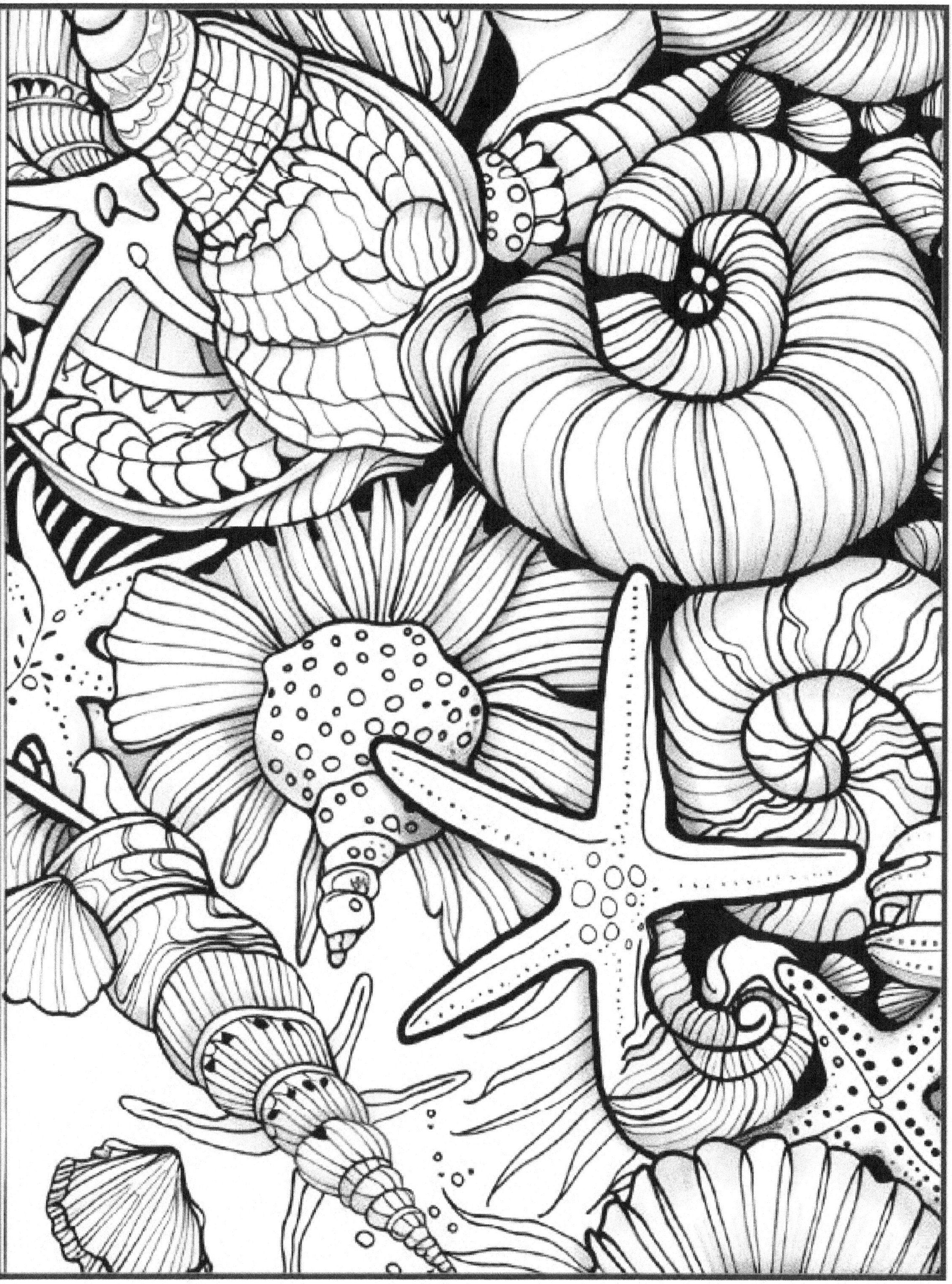

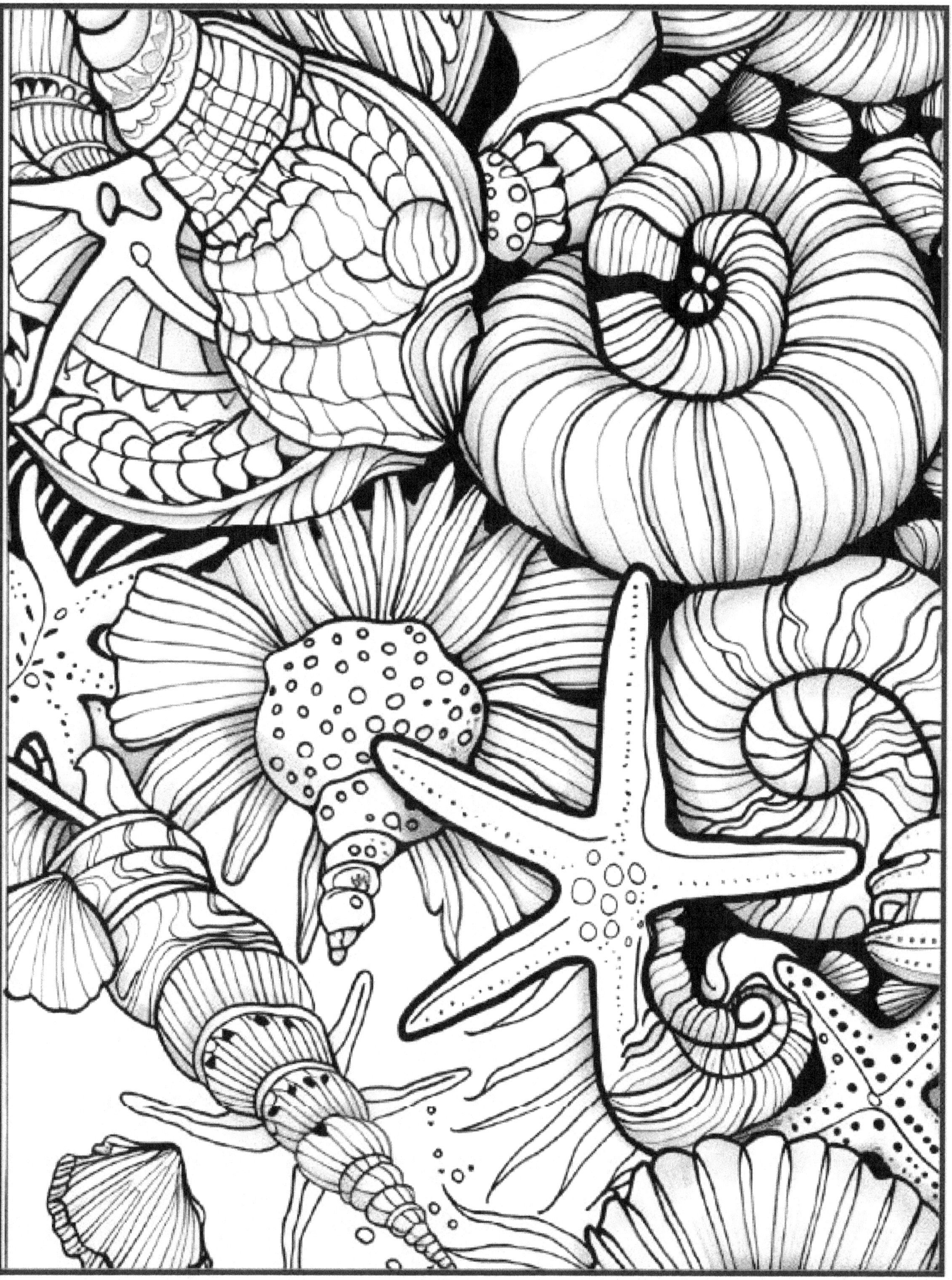

# ColorQuest Collections

**Fun and creative coloring books**

Calming | Relaxing | Stress Relief

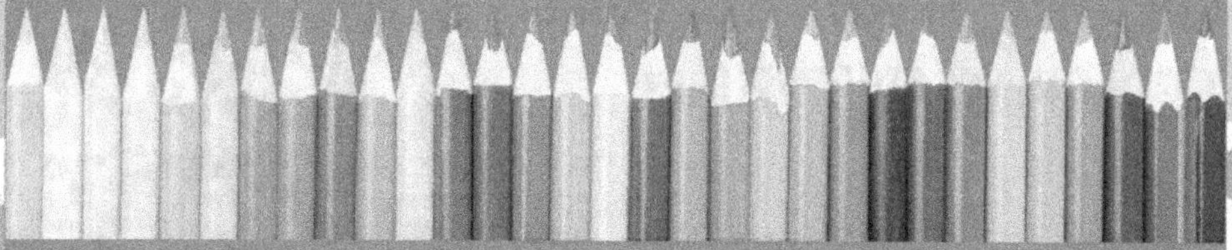

**For more fun and creative coloring books, search for ColorQuest Collections in your favorite bookstore!**

# Thank you

## PLEASE LEAVE US A REVIEW!

SCAN HERE

IF YOU ENJOYED THIS COLORING BOOK, PLEASE TAKE A MOMENT TO LEAVE A REVIEW. YOUR FEEDBACK HELPS US IMPROVE AND GUIDES OTHER CREATIVE SPIRITS TO THEIR PERFECT COLORING ADVENTURE!

FOR MORE CREATIVE COLORING BOOKS, PLEASE SEARCH FOR COLORQUEST COLLECTIONS IN YOUR FAVORITE BOOKSTORE!

## COLORQUEST COLLECTIONS

www.ingramcontent.com/pod-product-compliance
Lightning Source LLC
Chambersburg PA
CBHW082346220526
45470CB00008B/2657
*9798326720726*